feelingblue

A guide to handling teenage depression

Dr Daniel Fung and Carolyn Kee

with Dr Rebecca P Ang

Marshall Cavendish

Cover design: Benson Tan

Copyright © 2009 Marshall Cavendish International (Asia) Private Limited

Published by Marshall Cavendish Editions
An imprint of Marshall Cavendish International
1 New Industrial Road, Singapore 536196

Other Marshall Cavendish Offices:
Marshall Cavendish Ltd. 5th Floor, 32-38 Saffron Hill, London EC1N 8FH, UK • Marshall Cavendish Corporation. 99 White Plains Road, Tarrytown NY 10591-9001, USA • Marshall Cavendish International (Thailand) Co Ltd. 253 Asoke, 12th Flr, Sukhumvit 21 Road, Klongtoey Nua, Wattana, Bangkok 10110, Thailand • Marshall Cavendish (Malaysia) Sdn Bhd, Times Subang, Lot 46, Subang Hi-Tech Industrial Park, Batu Tiga, 40000 Shah Alam, Selangor Darul Ehsan, Malaysia

Marshall Cavendish is a trademark of Times Publishing Limited

National Library Board Singapore Cataloguing in Publication Data

Fung, Daniel.
Feeling blue : a guide to handling teenage depression / Daniel Fung and Carolyn Kee with Rebecca P. Ang. – Singapore : Marshall Cavendish Editions, c2009.
p. cm.
Includes bibliographical references.
ISBN-13 : 978-981-261-887-0

1. Depression in adolescence. 2. Youth – Suicidal behavior.
I. Ang, Rebecca (Rebecca Pei-Hui) II. Kee, Carolyn (Carolyn Hsiao Ying), 1972- III. Title.

RJ506.D4
616.85270083 -- dc22   OCN402048322

Printed in Singapore by Times Printers Pte Ltd

CONTENTS

FOREWORD

Depression is a serious problem that affects all ages of life, but in adolescence, it poses significant problems that can have a devastating impact on the individual. If unrecognised and untreated, the resulting complications include psychiatric disorders, unhealthy behaviours, violence and suicide.

The Centers for Disease Control and Prevention (CDC) in the US report that suicide is the third leading cause of death for 15 to 24-year-olds in the US. Fortunately teenage depression is highly treatable. The National Institute of Mental Health recommends not only medication, but a wide range of services such as family support services, education and behaviour management techniques in dealing with teenage depression.

This book is the first in local mental health care to provide a systematic introduction to the issue of teenage depression. It is valuable not only for various groups of professionals but also counsellors, educators and family members. The authors have successfully provided a pragmatic approach to a very serious problem.

A/Prof Rathi Mahendran
Senior Consultant Psychiatrist and Chairman
Medical Board
Institute of Mental Health, Singapore

To Deborah

To Gerald

PREFACE

We all want our children to have a happy childhood and to grow up into well-adjusted adults. Sadly for some children, their childhood is marred by anxiety and depression which may be brought on by such factors as stress from school, marital discord in the family or other relationship problems. The World Health Organisation (WHO) defines this impact of an illness on a person's daily life as "disease burden".

A study by the Ministry of Health in Singapore showed that more than 30% of disease burden for children aged below 15 were related to mental health conditions. Anxiety and depression ranked fifth in the top 10 causes of disease burden in children. It is up to adults to pick up on the signs and symptoms of depression among children and youths, and to help them accordingly. Sometimes, just being there to support and comfort them is all that they need, although in more severe cases, counselling and help from mental health professionals may be required.

This book puts together the experiences of patients, parents, teachers and mental health experts to help you better understand depression in children and adolescents. This book is intended for youths, parents and teachers so that they can look out for signs of depression in themselves, their friends, family members and students, and seek help, or provide the support and help needed.

We would like to thank Associate Professor Rathi Mahendran for writing the Foreword to this book, and Dr Cai Yiming for his helpful comments on the text. We would also like to thank Ms Chan Mei Chern and Ms Geraldine Wong for helping to set up REACH (Response, Early intervention and Assessment in Community mental Health) for which this book is intended to supplement. We would also like to extend our appreciation to our patients, their parents and the many teachers and school counsellors who have contributed to this book in one way or another.

Daniel Fung, Carolyn Kee and Rebecca Ang

01 SUICIDE: IS IT REAL?

Learning Points

- Suicide can happen to anyone.
- Suicide is not uncommon and can be prevented.
- Suicide prevention is the responsibility of everyone, not just the mental health professional.

Many people think that suicide is not something that will happen to them or their family. It only hits home when it happens to someone close to them. By then, it is too late to do anything about it.

No Signs Before Girl's Suicide

In 2001, a 10-year-old girl jumped off a block of flats[1]. The newspaper headline to the article on the case indicated that there were no signs for her suicide.

But there were in fact many signs which were uncovered during the coroner's inquiry. The primary school girl was a perfectionist and a quiet person who kept her feelings to herself. She was described by her teachers as being easily upset and pressured herself to do well. She was one of the top students in her school. Her parents said that she was stressed out by schoolwork and was afraid of being scolded. When stressed, she argued with her siblings. Two weeks before she took her own life, she expressed her intention to jump off from the block of flats where she lived, if she did not do well in her Higher Chinese test. And, she wanted to skip school on the day she killed herself.

Although suicide in young people is not common, it is heartbreaking to the people they leave behind. And it is not just their families, as their school teachers and classmates often feel guilty too. In some cases, they may also become depressed and suicidal themselves[2,3].

DEFINITIONS OF SUICIDE

Suicide is the intentional act of killing oneself. It is derived from the Latin word, *sui caedere*, which means to kill oneself. Suicide is often motivated by various external as well as internal factors. In a local study by Dr Chia Boon Hock, a psychiatrist in private practice who specialises in suicide studies, he noted that relationship problems with family and peers form the major cause for suicide[4]. But suicide is often the result of multiple reasons, rather than a single factor.

There are different terminologies to describe suicidal thinking and intent. The thought of suicide does not necessarily result in suicidal behaviour. Suicidal behaviour is sometimes arbitrarily defined as either self-harm or self-injury compared to the more serious definition of suicide attempt. How this is arrived at is however not clear. Today, some scientists use the term non-fatal self-harm which was previously described as parasuicide. In this context, the emphasis is on youths who do not wish to die, but engage in behaviours that cause anxiety and distress in others in their attempts to improve their own situation. Although there is a difference between the suicidal (serious intention to die) and suicide attempters (no death wish but a call for help), these adolescents share similar characteristics. There is a need to take suicide attempts seriously because of the potential fatal or harmful consequences resulting from these suicide attempts. As with the suicidal, suicide attempters need to be given appropriate help.

SUICIDE STATISTICS IN SINGAPORE YOUTHS

Suicide data is obtained through the Registry of Births and Deaths. It is often reported as a rate per 100,000 population in the age range. This is calculated by taking, for example, the number of suicides among youths aged between 15 and 19 years old, divided by the total number of youths in that age group.

Suicidal thoughts are common among the general population, even in children. Older children are more likely to harbour such thoughts especially in their early teens. Fortunately, in most cases, these ideas are not carried through to attempts and actual suicide. This is even higher in populations with mental illness[5].

Few attempts lead to actual suicide, but studies have shown that the lifetime prevalence of suicide attempts is between 3.5% and 11% and serious attempts is between 1% and 3% among children. Actual suicides are usually much lower[6,7,8].

In a recent local study of over 600 children aged six to 12 using a self-administered rating scale, 141 (22%) indicated that they wanted to kill themselves or had thoughts of killing themselves[9].

Suicide is a major cause of mortality in the young, even though it is the lowest in all age groups combined.

Chart 1: Distribution of suicide rates (per 100,000 population) by gender and age (2000)

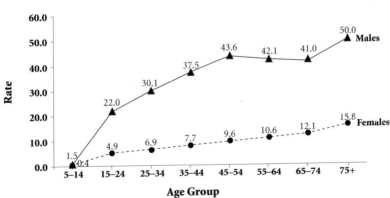

Charts 2 and 3: Singapore Suicide Rates (per 100,000 population)
by age from 1980 to 2007

Age 10 to 14

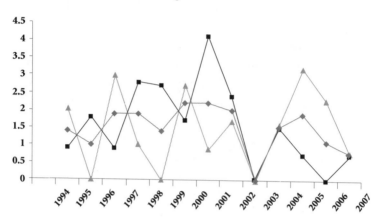

Age 15 to 19

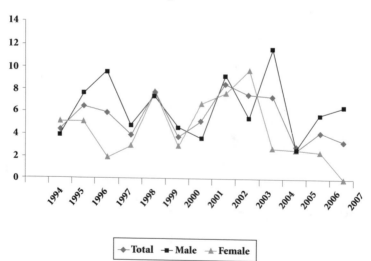

◆ Total ■ Male ▲ Female

The suicide rate among Singapore youths has fluctuated over the years and the trend showed an improvement with lower rates of suicide for those under the age of 19. This positive data hid a worrying trend of extremely young suicides which became more apparent in the past 10 years. Because of this, a national mental health prevention programme called "Mind Your Mind", was put in place.

THE MISCONCEPTIONS ABOUT SUICIDE

Many people have false ideas about suicide in young people. These myths, if not dispelled, stand in our way of reaching out and providing help to youths who are at risk of commiting suicide.

Misconception 1 Young people don't kill themselves.
Fact In North America, after accidents and homicides respectively, the third highest cause of death in young people between the ages of 15 and 24 is suicide. In many countries where the use of guns is prohibited, like Singapore, suicide deaths rank second, after deaths by accidents. This is the case even when suicide rates in general have fallen. For every 10 suicide attempts, at least one will actually be committed.

Misconception 2 You cannot stop someone who wants to commit suicide.
Fact As the psychological pain increases in young people, they tend to develop a narrow view of life and see no other way out of their problems. They are overwhelmed by a sense of helplessness and hopelessness, and see killing themselves as the only way out of their emotional trauma. But this is a temporary state. If they were given help to reduce their pain of living to a tolerable level, they would choose to live. And many children who have considered suicide, but did not go through with it, have gone on to lead fruitful and productive lives. Suicide is a permanent solution to what is usually a temporary problem.

Misconception 3 Young people who talk of suicide are only trying to get attention. Ignoring them is the best thing to do.

Fact Talking about suicide is a plea for help. They do not see other options to their problems and are desperate to the point of thinking of ending their lives. We should encourage them to talk further about what is troubling them and help them by getting them appropriate counselling assistance. We have to take them seriously, listen to them carefully and give them a chance to express their feelings.

Misconception 4 Young people who have attempted suicide before will not do it again.

Fact Within a year of a suicide attempt, the risk of a repeated attempt is high. A previous suicide attempt is regarded as an indicator of further attempts and studies have shown this to be true. A local study among those who were admitted to hospitals in 1987 for attempting suicide showed that about 0.5% of them eventually committed suicide within the same year.

Misconception 5 Talking about suicide or asking someone if they feel suicidal will encourage suicide attempts.

Fact Talking about suicide provides the opportunity for communication and often brings relief to those who are suicidal. Doing so allows them to share their feelings and reduce their fears. A simple inquiry asking them if they are thinking of ending their lives shows that you are concerned and care enough to listen. In fact, this is an important first step in helping to reduce suicidal despair. Anyone can take on this role, not just the professionals. But, how we handle such a situation is crucial and there are skills we can learn in order to effectively help those with suicidical tendencies.

Misconception 6 Improvement after a crisis means that the suicide risk is over.

Fact It is in the early period of improvement that suicidal persons can gain sufficient energy to turn their self-perceived hopeless thoughts and situations into destructive acts. In the three months following a suicide attempt, they are most at risk of completing the suicide. It is possible that they have made up their minds to end their lives and so they feel better and appear to have resolved their problems. This may explain why many suicides occur at this point of time. Therefore, we should continue to be vigilant even when the suicidal person begins to show signs of recovery and the crisis appears to be over.

Misconception 7 Suicidal young people are always angry when someone intervenes and they will hate that person after that.

Fact Suicidal young people are often defensive and sceptical that others are genuinely interested to help them. The initial behaviour of resisting help is to test how much people care and are prepared to help. Once the rapport and trust are formed, they would feel relieved to have others to share their psychological burden. Most of them, when questioned some time later, express gratitude for the intervention.

RISK FACTORS FOR SUICIDE

Suicidal youths may be encountered at the psychiatric emergency department, inpatient wards and outpatient clinics, or in counselling centres and in schools. Many studies have identified a number of different factors that contribute to these youths having suicidal thoughts.

Sociological Factors

This includes relationships within the family which can cause stress. Unhappy family situations such as parents who are perpetually quarrelling or going through a divorce can cause young people to feel guilty about what is happening, leading them to become depressed. High expectations by important adults in a youth's life have great impact on their feelings of adequacy and self worth. If parents and teachers continue to make unreasonable demands on the youth's performance, this could lead to acts of self destruction and suicide. Other reasons include poor school performance, criminal offences and illegal substance use which make them feel that they have let their parents down, driving them to become suicidal.

Psychological Factors

The internal mental processes in youths can sometimes drive them to suicidal thinking. This could be due to their personality characteristics such as being perfectionistic or highly anxious, causing them to feel easily overwhelmed and distressed. They may also be suffering from mental disorders like depression and anxiety, driving them to thoughts and acts of suicide.

Biological Factors

There are definite genetic risks to suicide, besides the environmental and psychological factors. Suicide runs in families not just because of environmental factors, but also due to specific brain chemistry that leads to such thoughts and acts. There have been suggestions that fluctuations in the brain chemical, serotonin, may in fact cause suicidal acts.

MEDIA REPORTING OF YOUTH SUICIDE

News of suicides are sometimes reported with intimate details of the person's life and method of suicide. There is evidence that some forms of non-fictional newspaper and television coverage of suicide are associated with higher suicide rates and the impact appears to be strongest among young people.

One of the earliest associations between the media and suicide involves Johann Wolfgang von Goethe's novel, The Sorrows of Young Werther, published in 1774. In the novel, the protagonist commits suicide by shooting himself as a result of an ill-fated relationship. Shortly after the book was released, there were many reports of young men using the same method to commit suicide. The term "Werther effect" has thus been used to describe copycat suicide. The degree of publicity given to a suicide story has been directly related to the number of subsequent suicides. Reports of suicides involving celebrities also have a particularly strong impact.

ASSESSING SUICIDE RISK

For any risk assessment to be clinically meaningful, various factors should be taken into account. These include the level of suicide intent, the severity of depression, the degree of hopelessness, the impact of life events and how life-threatening the attempt is. For the lay-person, the simplest way to do this is to use a rating scale to help measure the likelihood of a person committing suicide.

In Singapore, our school counsellors are taught to look out for signs of suicide through regular training by the Ministry of Education's Guidance Branch. In clinical settings, the Beck's Suicidal Intent Scale is widely used although the Singapore Armed Forces has its own variation of this scale. Rating scales, however, should serve only as guides. Clinical assessment of the risk must come from the person who is seeing the youth.

An Example of Suicide Risk Assessment[10]

Here is an example of how suicide risk can be assessed. Ask yourself or the person who is suicidal, "Are you feeling so depressed that you want to kill yourself?" If the answer to this question is "Yes", follow up with these questions:

1. Is this unhappy feeling so strong that you wish you were dead?
2. How often have you been having these thought?
3. What happened recently to make you feel this way?
4. On a scale of 1 to 10, how strong is your desire to take your own life?
5. What will it take for you to feel better?
6. Have you thought of how you want to kill yourself?
7. Is the method easily available?
8. Have you planned when you want to do this?
9. Have you tried to harm or kill yourself before?
10. Did things change as a result of these attempts?
11. Is there anything that will stop you from killing yourself?
12. Allow yourself to look into the future—what are the things that you can look forward to?

Learning Points

- Children and adolescents can be depressed.
- Parents can train children to be resilient to protect them from depression and to be able to handle stress better.
- Depression is a medical condition and requires medical evaluation.
- Depressed children and adolescents may go unnoticed because they are quiet and withdrawn.
- Depression can lead to suicide.
- Depression can be treated. Good relationships can protect against depression.

"I Don't Understand What She Wants!"

Karen is a 12-year-old girl who jumped off from the second floor of the HDB apartment block where she lives and broke her legs. While warded in the hospital, she expressed her fears of not doing well in school and about the Primary School Leaving Examination (PSLE). Jumping off from the block was her attempt at avoiding the disappointment of failing. In response, Karen's mother said she provided Karen with all that she needed. But children need more than physical and material comfort. They need to feel loved unconditionally. Parents need to spend time with their children and be there for them especially when they are under stress, such as during examination periods.

WHY DO CHILDREN BECOME DISTRESSED?

Mental health problems in children are relatively common. Depression in children and adolescents is an important public health issue. Between 5% and 26% of children may require help at some time. These periods of distress can be defined as disturbances in the areas of relationship, feelings, behaviour or development. But it is only in severe cases that they will need to see a psychiatrist, as many of these problems can be handled and resolved by family doctors, counsellors and social workers. The most common cause of death in Singapore youths, besides accidents, is suicide, and many suicidal acts are related to low mood and depression. Although the rate of suicide in Singapore youths is low compared to that in developed countries, it has been creeping up over the last 30 years.

Children and Their Emotions

Children have feelings and emotions. Their phases of development affect the way they respond to emotional experiences. For example, very young children may not have the language to describe their feelings. Hence they will act out their emotions. A baby who is hungry will cry out for food. A child who is frustrated will throw a tantrum. As children get older, they gradually learn to express their feelings through words. Unfortunately, some parents choose to ignore or brush off what their children have to say. When a child tells his parents, "I am afraid", his parents may respond by saying "Why should you be afraid? There is nothing to fear!" Such responses may in time cause these children to hide their feelings. And as they are not able to say what they feel, they may resort to acting up physically. How children express themselves depend on their social and cultural backgrounds and their language capability. In a study of Singaporean children's expression of depression, it was evident that the reactions of an adult, who played an important role in the child's life (such as the child's mother or a teacher), affected the child's emotional state. Depending on the relationship they share, this can lead to feelings of depression and sadness[1].

PREVENTING DEPRESSION

Prevention is always better than cure. So how can we prevent children from falling into depression? The answer is two-fold. Firstly, children should be protected from the potential causes of depression such as the environmental stressors described earlier. Secondly, children must be brought up to be resilient against stress. Such resilience requires that children be taught competency skills early to develop self-reliance and independence. Problem-solving instead of avoidance of failure is another necessary skill that will improve their resilience.

How Can Parents of Children with Emotional Disorders Help Their Children?

The basic principles of good parenting include understanding your child, understanding yourself, understanding how you and your child interact, and having a variety of techniques to manage your child.

- **Understanding your child**

  You know your child best. Different parenting techniques work for different children. Handle your child according to his temperament and behaviour and find the way that best suits your child. The important thing is to recognise that your child has feelings too.

- **Understanding yourself**

  Be aware of your own emotions. If you are easily stressed, it would be difficult to look after your own children. Take as an analogy, the aircraft safety procedure of fitting the oxygen mask on yourself before attending to your child. Taking care of yourself is the first step to being a good parent. If you cannot handle your own emotions, you will not be able to help your child.

- **Understanding techniques**

  A variety of techniques are available to help parents deal with their children. Behaviour modification is the technique of reinforcing good behaviour and playing down bad behaviour. This is commonly used with young children who are responsive to rewards and punishments. Older children may need more subtle handling using responsibilities and consequences. Read up on different parenting techniques and apply them to your child, bearing in mind the first two points above. All children need discipline, but discipline does not mean physical punishment. It simply means being firm, consistent, loving, and considerate of their feelings.

HOW COMMON IS CHILDHOOD DEPRESSION?

If your child's sadness is prolonged and it is affecting his relationship with the people around him, as well as his daily activities like eating, sleeping and playing, he is likely to be depressed. Depression in children and adolescents is not easily identified and can often go unnoticed. If depression is not well treated, it may continue into adulthood.

Prevalence of depression depends on how it is defined and how it was screened. A local community survey using a locally derived rating scale for depression in adolescents showed that depression occurs in 2% to 2.5% of the adolescent population[2]. A larger survey showed that up to 17.2% of primary school children have symptoms associated with depression[3]. Based on the assumption that about 10% of children may have depressive symptoms, this implies that about 100,000 children and teenagers may be depressed and more than 10,000 may actually suffer from depressive disorder. Western studies have shown that at any one time, about 2% to 8% of children and adolescents can have a depressive disorder, and one in every six people, including adults, may have some type of depression in their lifetime. There has been no survey of younger children in Singapore, but several studies put the occurrence of depression among this age group as lower. Most of the depressed young children tend to come from socially deprived backgrounds and may be victims of child abuse and neglect.

UNDERSTANDING YOUTHS WITH DEPRESSION

There are three critical differences between youths and adults which must be taken into consideration when discussing the problem of depression and suicide.

Youths Are Developing

The first is that youths are still growing and developing. Their needs and wants change from day to day, week to week, month to month and year to year. This constant change presents a dynamic challenge for adults and it is not surprising that these roller coaster moods can cause youths to go from extreme happiness to the depths of depression. The same can be said of feelings of wanting to die. Several surveys have shown that young people think of dying at some point in their growing years. A local study of primary school children[3] showed that about a third of them had had thoughts of dying in the past six months, but only less than 5% of parents, and even fewer teachers, were aware of it. For the majority of youths, however, these thoughts are only temporary and they will pass. The features of true depressive disorder, which warrants attention, will be highlighted later in this chapter.

Youths Are Not Masters of Their Own Fate

The second important difference is that youths have little, if any control, over their lives in many instances. Even older teenagers often find that parents, guardians and other adults control their lives by dictating terms and conditions. This is not a bad thing in itself, but it may present a challenge when the circumstances become unbearable to the teenager, such as in the situation where the youth is abused. Recognising that youths have rights does not necessarily mean that they get to exercise those rights. In fact, many youths (in the younger age group) may actually be so helpless in their situation that they contemplate suicide on a regular basis. This is most prominent in situations where youths are abused by adults or their peers, in the form of bullying.

Youths Crave Good Relationships

This third element is quite critical and if youths are faced with difficult relationships, whether with their parents or peers, they are at a higher risk of falling into depression and subsequently, attempting or committing suicide. Youths consistently rate relationships as the most important aspect of their lives. This is in keeping with an important adolescent challenge of developing a good sense of self-efficacy and self-esteem. Relationships help to validate the feelings of the youths toward themselves. Good relationships make youths feel good about themselves, that they are loved. Bad relationships make them feel that they are unloved and unwanted.

HOW IS DEPRESSION DEFINED IN THE YOUNG?

All of us feel sadness at some points in our lives. We may have failed a test or lost our favourite pet, and we feel sad. Such sadness is normal. Depressed mood is therefore not a disorder, but can be a risk factor for it. A child who is always sad will have a greater chance of developing a depressive disorder. A more serious emotional disorder may occur when the child has symptoms that impair his function to some degree. Besides feeling depressed and sad, the child may be anxious, have problems dealing with school and classmates and generally not feel good.

In psychiatric practice, depressive disorders are persistent sad feelings that affect children or adolescents in ways that they cannot handle. They may not enjoy activities which they usually enjoy, they may not sleep or eat well, they may feel tired or bad tempered and they may not be able to concentrate on their studies. They may be so overwhelmed by these feelings that they start having thoughts of dying. Because children find it hard to describe their feelings, depressive disorder may result in certain behaviours such as refusing to go to school. Some children may also develop headaches or stomachaches.

The prevalence of depressive mood is always higher than the prevalence of depressive disorder, the latter being a more serious condition. A simple way to identify depressive disorder is to consider five main elements:
- Depressive mood is severe and intense
- It is persistent
- It occurs in many situations (pervasive)
- It is inappropriate and inexplicable
- It greatly impairs the child's ability to function normally

The symptoms of depression are similar in adults and the young, but atypical features are more common in the young. Children and adolescents may present with irritable rather than depressed mood and have greater sleeping complaints. In children, depression can affect both boys and girls. Some studies also indicate that adolescents who are depressed may have an increased occurrence of hallucinatory experiences such as hearing voices of people accusing them of being bad[4]. In Singapore, preliminary studies seem to indicate that children with depression have greater concern about the way they relate to people important to them, such as their parents and teachers.

Table 1: The Classic Symptoms of Depression and Questions to Help Identify Them

Symptoms	Questions
Persistent sad or irritable mood	How has your child been feeling lately?
	Does your child cry for no reason?
	How often does this happen?
	How long does it last?
Loss of interest in activities once enjoyed (Anhedonia)	Has your child lost interest in his usual activities?
	Does he derive less pleasure from things he used to enjoy?
Difficulty sleeping or oversleeping	How has your child been sleeping?
	How does that compare with his normal sleep pattern?
Significant change in appetite or body weight	Has there been any change in your child's appetite or weight?
Decreased energy	Have you noticed a decrease in your child's energy level?
Increased or decreased psychomotor activity	Has your child been feeling fidgety or is he having problems sitting still?
	Has your child slowed down or become withdrawn?
Decreased concentration	Has your child been having trouble concentrating?
	Does he find it harder to make decisions than before?
	Does the school teacher complain that your child is always in a world of his own?
Feelings of worthlessness or inappropriate guilt	Does your child blame himself when things go wrong?
	Does your child apologise for things that are not a result of his fault?
Recurrent thoughts of death or suicide	Has your child expressed that life is not worth living or that he would be better off dead?
	Has he been sharing any thoughts about killing himself?
	Have you found notes expressing suicidal ideas?

Less common symptoms of depression include:
- Frequent vague, non-specific physical complaints
- Refusal to go to school for no apparent reason
- Poor academic performance
- Feeling that no one (such as parents, teachers and peers) cares
- Emotional outbursts
- Frequent complaints of being bored
- Lack of interest in playing with friends
- Social isolation
- Fear of death
- Extreme sensitivity to rejection or failure
- Increased irritability, anger or hostility
- Reckless behaviour
- Difficulty with relationships
- Addictive behaviours such as overuse of the computer and Internet

Obviously such symptoms can occur in a variety of situations and it may be necessary to seek professional help to determine the cause.

MISCONCEPTIONS ABOUT DEPRESSION IN THE YOUNG

Misconception 1 It is normal for teens to be moody.
Fact This is definitely untrue. Feeling sad is different from having a depressive disorder. Normal mood swings of adolescence will not impair the person's function and cause them to commit suicide.

Misconception 2 Depressed people are mentally weak and need to pull themselves together.
Fact Depression is an illness that needs treatment. Teenagers with this illness cannot just pull themselves together and get well. They need help.

Misconception 3 Talking about depression only makes it worse.
Fact Part of helping children and adolescents with depression is to allow

them to talk through their problems and help them to approach the relevant issues such as problems in their thinking process or the difficulties in their interpersonal relationships. Talking about depression makes it better.

Misconception 4 People who talk about suicide don't commit suicide.
Fact In a local study of teens who committed suicide in 2003, it was found that about half of them had written suicide notes. In a much larger study by Dr Chia Boon Hock, a local psychiatrist, many depressed teens also inform people close to them of their sadness and intention to kill themselves[5].

Misconception 5 Telling on a friend is betraying their trust.
Fact If someone needs help, they will ask for it. Helping a friend who is depressed is not betraying their trust. When a child or adolescent is depressed, they see the world in a different light and without help, they have very little chance of getting out of it.

CAUSES OF DEPRESSION IN YOUTHS

Environmental Factors
Besides genetic causes such as a family history of depression or suicide, a child who is temperamentally more anxious or prone to anxiety may also develop depression if the anxiety is not well treated. In addition, perfectionistic character traits may also make a child more easily depressed. Depression can be caused by stress resulting from environmental factors such as:
- Parents going through a divorce or in conflict
- Deteriorating school performance
- Abuse by family members
- Coexisting medical conditions, such as chronic problems and juvenile diabetes
- Death of a parent/parents
- Poor relationships with peers and bullying by peers
- Facing serious punishment for delinquent acts
- Substance abuse

Our local studies on depressed children showed that interpersonal factors are the major causes of depression. When the child feels that the important caregivers (such as parents and teachers) in their lives think poorly of them, they tend to become depressed.

Medical Factors

It is important for a doctor to assess a depressed child or adolescent as some medical conditions can cause depressive-like symptoms. For example, a child with hypothyroidism may be lethargic and slow, giving the impression that he is depressed. Other medical mimics may include infections, neurological disorders as well as other rare conditions. The intake of certain medications may also cause depressive-like symptoms in children and adolescents. These medical mimics of depression are listed in the table below.

Table 2: The Medical Mimics of Depression

Infections	Neurological Disorders	Endocrine	Medications	Others
Infectious mononucleosis	Epilepsy	Diabetes	Benzodiazepines	Alcohol abuse
Influenza	Post-concussion	Cushing's	Cimetidine	Drug abuse
Encephalitis	Strokes	Addison's	Aminophylline	Electrolyte abnormality
Pneumonia	Multiple Schlerosis	Hypo-thyroidism	Anti-convulsants	Failure to thrive
TB hepatitis	Huntington's Disease	Hyper-thyroidism	Clonidine	Anemia
Syphilis		Hyperpara-thyroidism	Anti-hypertensives	Lupus
AIDS		Hypo-pituitarism		Wilson's
				Porphyria
				Uremia

TREATMENT OF DEPRESSION IN YOUTHS

Children and adolescents with depression should be encouraged to talk about their feelings. Parents and teachers should acknowledge these feelings, try to lessen their stress and help them to develop coping skills. The key to helping depressed youths is in increasing their self esteem, developing coping skills to handle stress and adapting to the changes in life and improving relationships with family members and peers.

One of the well studied methods for helping depressed youths is Cognitive Behaviour Therapy (CBT). CBT has been shown to be an effective treatment that is maintained over time. Other forms of talking therapies (psychotherapy) used in youths include psychodynamic psychotherapy, interpersonal therapy, family therapy, supportive psychotherapy and group psychotherapy. Use of medications should be cautious and not necessarily be first-line treatment. Medications shown to be useful in adults may not be as well tolerated in children. Medications are usually indicated for patients with severe depression, have psychotic symptoms or have failed psychotherapy. Use of Electro-Convulsive Therapy (ECT) is rarely used but it has been shown to be safe in adolescents[6]. This involves sending an electric current to the brain to correct the chemical imbalance caused by the depression.

Medications

Between 1950 and 1960, the advent of medications for treating what used to be thought of as incurable, started a revolution of psychotropic medications. The use of these medications for youths has taken off only recently. However, this has also created concern about the use of medications and, in North America, this has created a backlash of negative public opinion.

Most of the evidence on the use of medications in emotional and behavioural disorders is derived from adults and the evidence for use in children is incomplete and need further studies. With this in mind, medications for use in depressed and suicidal youths must be tempered by the potential risk that medications may pose.

Guidelines to the Use of Medications to Treat Depression

- Start at the lowest possible dose and gradually increase the dosage over time as this will reduce the risk of side effects.
- Use single medications rather than combinations. Multiple medications may interact with one another and cause side effects.
- Discuss the use of medications with family members and teachers so that they can look out for side effects and ensure adherence to treatment, and make sure that the patient takes the prescribed medication.
- Allow enough time for the medication to take effect. The effects of the medication are is not immediate and may take one to two weeks before a change is noted.
- Be aware of the common and serious side effects of the medications and inform your doctor if you notice them.

Table 3: Medications Used for Depressed Youths

Medications	Indications	Examples
Serotonin-specific reuptake inhibitors (SSRI)	Depression and anxiety disorders including obsessive compulsive disorders	Fluoxetine Fluvoxamine Sertraline Escitalopram Paroxetine
Tricyclic antidepressants	Depression and anxiety disorders Bedwetting (Nocturnal enuresis) School refusal	Imipramine Amitriptyline
Specific-noradrenergic reuptake inhibitors (SNRI)	Second line treatment for depression	Venlafaxine
Benzodiazepines	For insomnia, agitation and anxiety	Lorazepam Diazepam
Typical antipsychotics	Second line treatment for anxiety and depression	Haloperidol Chlorpromazine
Atypical antipsychotics	Second line treatment for intellectually inpaired, depressed Clozapine shown to reduce suicidality in adults	Risperidone Olanzapine Clozapine
Lithium	Bipolar Disorder	For prevention and treatment of illness relapse

Anticonvulsants	Bipolar Disorder (Rapid cycling type)	Sodium Valproate
		Carbamazepine
Stimulants	Not indicated	Methylphenidate
		Atomoxetine

How Medications Work in Suicidal and Depressed Youths

As our understanding of emotional disorders improve, there is evidence that brain chemicals responsible for transmitting impulses play an important role. These brain chemicals are called neurotransmitters and the most common are serontonin, dopamine and norepinephrine. Medications that are used to treat depression work on serotonin and norepinephrine. However, these important neurotransmitters have other functions too. When a child takes these medications, they can cause side effects. It is therefore important for adults and older youths to be aware of the side effects of such medications.

Side Effects from the Use of Anti-depressants

The most important side effects in the use of antidepressants are:

Sedation

This is a common side effect which can affect a child's ability to concentrate in school. However, the dosage of the medication can be reduced to lessen the sedative effects or it can be taken at night before going to bed. The most common medications that cause sedation are the benzodiazepines.

Serotonin syndrome

This is rare in childhood but may occur if SSRIs (serotonin-specific reuptake inhibitors) are used especially with multiple medications. The common symptoms include restlessness and agitation, rapid heartbeat, headaches, shivering, confusion and fits.

Other side effects

The commonly seen side effects from Anticholinergic drugs are mild dryness of the mouth and blurring of vision. They may occasionally also cause constipation and lead to difficulties in passing urine.

Fears of addiction

Generally, antidepressants are not addictive although benzodiazepines can be, if prescribed for long periods. However, although there are no physical dependency symptoms, some youths on antidepressants (primarily the SSRIs) may develop withdrawal symptoms which can manifest as severe anxiety. One way to reduce this is to reduce the SSRIs gradually over time.

Fears of suicide

Recent public concern about psychotropic medications causing suicide is the result of an ongoing debate about the use of SSRIs in youths. In 2003, the Medicines and Healthcare Products Regulatory Agency (MHRA) in the UK found that all SSRIs were unfavourable except for Fluoxetine based on five positive medication studies and three failed or negative medication studies. This just means that of all the studies done, some have shown that SSRIs are useful while others have not. It is important to recognise that clinical trials (or studies) tend to exclude severely suicidal individuals and their effectiveness in reducing or increasing risks of suicide are difficult to prove experimentally. In fact, epidemiological evidence in North America suggests that there is an overall reduction in suicide rates with the introduction of SSRIs. Autopsy data on youths who have committed suicide suggest that those prescribed antidepressants do not always take them. Case studies and numerical increases in suicidal behaviour in clinical trials are based on retrospective data, and there were no suicides in more than 2,000 subjects studied who took the medication that they were prescribed. It is therefore important to note that suicide as a side effect of medication is generally unfounded and if a child or adolescent requires medication, it means that the depression is severe.

Fears of overdosage

Overdosage is a frequent form of a suicide attempt. As some antidepressants are potentially lethal in overdose, there is a fear that suicides may result from the very medications used to treat the depression. It is important that parents administer medications to depressed and suicidal youths. As the medications take time to work, this needs to be done in the first one to two weeks of starting the medication to prevent a self administered overdose.

Name of Medication	Common Dose for Treatment	Contraindication	Common Side Effects	Other Comments
Fluoxetine (Prozac)	20 mg in the morning and up to 60 mg per day	Hypersensitivity to MAOIs, mania and hypomania, liver disease	Agitation, insomnia, drowsiness, diarrhoea, gastrointestinal upset, headaches, skin rash	This medication has the most evidence for use in childhood. The long time it stays in the body is a disadvantage.
Imipramine	0.5 mg/kg/day Maximum dose 100 mg/day	Hypersensitivity, narrow angle glaucoma, hypomania and mania, caution with epilepsy, hyperthyroidism, cardiac disease	Dry mouth, sedation, urinary retention	Do not use with SSRIs (as they reduce the metabolism of imipramine)
Lorazepam	0.25 to 0.5 mg per dose Maximum of 2 mg per day	Hypersensitivity, Narrow angle glaucoma	Sedation Respiratory depression in high dose	
Haloperidol	0.07 mg/ kg /day Maximum of 0.2 mg/kg/day in divided doses	Hypersensitivity, blood dyscrasias, Severe extrapyramidal side-effects (EPSE) with other antipsychotics	Sedation EPSE	Do not combine with Lithium
Risperidone (Risperdal)	0.015 mg/kg/day Maximum of 0.05 mg/kg/day in divided doses	Hypersensitivity	Weight gain EPSE in high doses	
Clozapine (Clozaril)	3 mg/kg/day Maximum of 8 mg/kg/day in divided doses	Previous blood dyscrasias, allergy and cardiac disease	Agranulocytosis in 1–2% Seizures, tachycardia	Need to do blood monitoring in the first 18 weeks of treatment

RESOURCES FOR HELPING DEPRESSED YOUTHS

Apart from confiding in adults they are familiar with when they are feeling down or depressed, there are helplines specially for children and adolescents. For older children and adolescents, there are self-help books and websites which they can turn to. Details can be found in Chapter 7.

03 A YOUNG PERSON'S GUIDE TO MANAGING DEPRESSION

Learning Points

Depression can be helped by:
- Self-monitoring
- Making concrete plans
- Dealing with negative thoughts

This chapter is for youths and their friends to learn how they can help themselves. Our experience in working with youths has shown us that sometimes it is better for the youths to manage themselves rather than rely on well meaning adults.

SELF-MONITORING

Instead of being driven to despair and thinking of ways of committing suicide, write down your feelings in your diary, notebook or blog. Keeping a record of your feelings both when you are happy and when you are feeling down, helps you to have control over your emotions.

Self-monitoring of Suicidal Thoughts

This means observing your pattern of activities during the period when you feel like killing yourself. Record what you do hour by hour. This may sound tedious, but it will help you regain perspective. Give each activity a rating between 0 and 10 for how you feel.

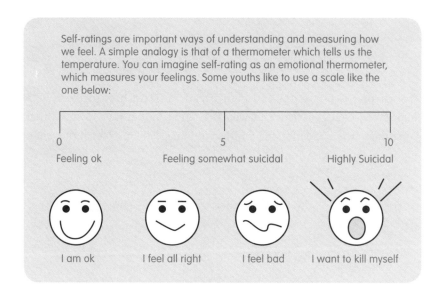

Self-ratings are important ways of understanding and measuring how we feel. A simple analogy is that of a thermometer which tells us the temperature. You can imagine self-rating as an emotional thermometer, which measures your feelings. Some youths like to use a scale like the one below:

0	5	10
Feeling ok	Feeling somewhat suicidal	Highly Suicidal
I am ok	I feel all right	I feel bad	I want to kill myself

Problems with Self-monitoring

Many teenagers tell us that they find monitoring useless and tedious. In fact, when asked what they did the whole day, they easily sum it up in a word, "nothing". This is because when we are asked to describe mundane daily activities such as sitting on a chair or watching the news on television, it is regarded as "nothing".

Another common problem is under-estimating achievements in overcoming obstacles. If you successfully coped with the suicidal thoughts by using distractions and doing something, it is helpful to acknowledge it. For example, "I was feeling depressed, so I went for a walk and I felt better."

It is important to rate feelings as soon as you experience them and not procrastinate. If you say "I will rate myself later" and then allow the bad feelings to cloud your day, things would seem much worse than they really were. Suicidal feelings fluctuate and by rating your feelings regularly, you can see that there are moments when you feel better. Without this rating, such moments might go unnoticed.

MAKING CONCRETE PLANS

Besides regular self-monitoring, it helps to plan your day and week in advance. As suicidal feelings become pronounced when one loses control, planning gives you a sense of control and prevents your feelings from controlling you.

1. Plan Activities

Think of "feel good" activities that you can do to start off the day. You may want to treat yourself to your favourite food or go somewhere you like. If you enjoy physical activities, playing a game, going for a run or a swim can perk you up.

This planning can be done either at the end of the day (for the next day) or the beginning of each day. Reminders to plan are useful, and you can stick up notes for yourself or use electronic reminders.

Keep a balance of fun things to do as well as chores and duties. This balance is important so that you can enjoy the day without feeling that nothing has been accomplished.

Keep yourself busy to distract you from your depression and any thoughts of suicide, but don't overwhelm yourself by trying to do too many things.

2. Record What You Do

Make it a habit to write everything that you do in a small notebook and rate your activities. The book also serves as a reminder of learning points and other useful tips which you can share with your therapist or counsellor and for your own recollection.

3. Review What You Have Done

In therapy, this is frequently done but teenagers can do this on a daily or weekly basis. This will enable them to review their progress and feelings by referring to their records. Here is a list of things that should be included in your concrete plans.

- Make a list of the things you need to do
- Prioritise them—do the important ones first
- Break the tasks into steps
- Rehearse the steps mentally
- Write down negative thoughts (see the next section for details)
- Write down what you did
- Review what you did

GETTING STARTED

Getting started is difficult. But if you procrastinate, the things you need to do start piling up, and you end up feeling discouraged. This in turn will make you feel hopeless, more depressed and even suicidal. Don't be too rigid, don't worry or fret if things don't go as planned or as well as you wanted them to be. Get going anyway, and expect the unexpected.

- Just get going—don't let things pile up
- Don't worry if things don't go as planned
- Be prepared that things may go wrong—expect the unexpected
- Don't stop when it gets tough

DEALING WITH NEGATIVE THOUGHTS

Negative thoughts are the thoughts which make us feel bad about ourselves. These thoughts can occur in many different situations. They can occur without any warning, especially if we are anxious or have a temperament that makes us think of the worst rather than the best. They can come when we are feeling down and can be part of a vicious cycle that leads to depression and thoughts of suicide. Negative thoughts alone do not make us feel bad if they are counterbalanced with reality and positive thoughts. However, negative thoughts can be so overpowering that good thoughts are crowded out. Common negative thoughts that bring about a downward spiral of negative feelings include over-generalisations, all-or-nothing thinking, selective thinking, self-referencing and jumping to conclusions.

Over-generalisations are negative thoughts associated with making sweeping statements based on single occurrences of events. For example, "My teacher scolded me for not handing in homework on time. She hates me. Everyone hates me!"

All-or-nothing thinking are negative thoughts that occur in extremes and tend to be associated with perfectionism. For example, "If I can't get full marks, there is no point in taking the exams."

Selective thinking is associated with remembering only the negative aspects of experiences. For example, "I did nothing at all today that I enjoyed."

Self-referencing is a form of negative thinking associated with believing that everyone is referring to them in a negative way. For example, "He looks angry. He must be angry with me."

Jumping to conclusions are negative thoughts about poor outcomes without considering other alternatives. For example, "She didn't say hello. She must hate me because I am a bad person!"

There are some things that you can do to overcome negative thoughts. You may want to put these steps down on a card or key them into your handphone, so you can refer to it anytime when you find yourself having negative thoughts.

The steps can be easily remembered by the mnemonic BAT.

Step 1: Being Aware

Recognising that a negative thought has crept into your consciousness requires effort. The body reacts to negative thoughts through your feelings. If you are feeling down, disheartened or sad, there is usually a negative thought sneaking about in your head. Step 1 can be broken down into several smaller steps using a table like the one below:

Date/ Time	Feelings	Situation	Negative Thoughts	Your Answer	The Outcome

In our clinic, we often help teenagers recognise their bad feelings so that they know that negative thoughts are around. There are two ways of recognising bad feelings. One is simply knowing and recording the bad feeling such as "feeling sad", although this makes it hard to identify subtle differences in the intensity of the feeling. The other way is to have a rating for the feeling, which is more useful. To do this, you simply do the self-monitoring exercise mentioned earlier and record it with a rating (from 0 to 10, where 0 means feeling fine and 10 means feeling very sad). For example:

Date/ Time	Feelings	Situation	Negative Thoughts	Your Answer	The Outcome
2/2/09 4 pm	Feeling down Rating = 8	Came home from school			

After recognising the unpleasant feelings, you will need to identify the negative thoughts that are occurring. Negative thoughts can be described in words or expressed with a doodle. The key is to know the thoughts and have them recorded. If you are busy, make a note of it so that you will be able to return to it for a more detailed review. It is important to record the thought(s) as accurately as possible. For example:

Date/ Time	Feelings	Situation	Negative Thoughts	Your Answer	The Outcome
2/2/09 4 pm	Feeling down Rating = 8	Came home from school	Today is a wasted day, I did nothing useful. I don't remember anything I learned. Why do I bother to go to school?		

It is not always easy to recognise negative thoughts. Some teenagers who are suicidal, find it hard to identify these negative thoughts and deal with them. Instead, they can only think of taking their own lives to escape from their emotional pain. It is important to give yourself a time limit to think of distressing thoughts. You can do this if you have a daily plan of absorbing activities to take your mind off such thoughts.

Step 2: Answering Negative Thoughts

Steps 2 and 3 are two of the common alternatives of handling negative thoughts. In Step 2, it is a form of challenging the thought (in your own mind) with realistic but logical and helpful thoughts. Here are some questions you can ask yourself when faced with negative thoughts.

- What is the evidence?
- Am I confusing a thought with a fact?
- Am I jumping to conclusions?
- What are the alternative views?
- Am I assuming that my views are the only possible explanation?
- What is the effect of thinking the way I do?
- Do negative thoughts help or hinder me?
- What are the advantages and disadvantages of thinking this way?
- Am I asking questions that have no answers?
- What thinking errors am I making? (For example, jumping to conclusions, over-generalising, taking responsibility for things that are not your fault etc.)

- Am I thinking in all-or-nothing terms?
- Am I using ultimatum words in my thinking? (Always, never, everyone, no one, everything, nothing)
- Am I condemning myself as a whole person based on a single event?
- Am I concentrating on my weakness and forgetting my strengths?
- Am I blaming myself for something that is really not my fault?
- Am I taking things personally which have little to do with me?
- Am I expecting myself to be perfect?
- Am I using a double standard?
- Am I only paying attention to the bad side of things?
- Am I over-estimating the chances of failure or disaster?
- Am I exaggerating the importance of events?
- Am I fretting about the way things ought to be instead of accepting them as they are?

My Classmates Hate Me!

A teenager once told me that his classmates in his new school did not like him. He came to that conclusion because they did not talk to him in class. When I asked him if there were any reasons he could think of for them not talking to him, he came up with a few reasons—they were not supposed to talk in class, he did not introduce himself and he shied away from looking at anyone which might have given them the impression that he himself was unfriendly.

Here is an example of the completed diary where the negative thoughts have been answered with logical thoughts.

Date/ Time	Feelings	Situation	Negative Thoughts	Your Answer	The Outcome
2/2/09 4 pm	Feeling down Rating = 8	Came home from school	Today is a wasted day, I did nothing useful. I don't remember anything I learned. Why do I bother to go to school?	My time table showed that I attended lessons and I made some notes with worksheets. I read through my worksheets and it wasn't as hard as I imagined.	I feel better Rating = 4

Common Problems with Answering Negative Thoughts

- Lack of practice: Dealing with negative thoughts takes some practice. Over time, you will find that it becomes easier. Keep trying and don't give up.

- Extreme distress: In moments of extreme sadness or emotional distress, it is difficult to think clearly. Make notes and write down what is going through your mind and return to answer those negative thoughts when you are calmer.

- Being a perfectionist: Everyone makes mistakes. And you are no different. Allow yourself to make mistakes and learn from them. Your diary is not meant to be a bestseller. It is to help you change the way you think and feel.

- Putting yourself down: Stop criticising yourself. Instead, give yourself time to learn to recognise your thoughts and record them conscientiously.

- Repeating thoughts: It is discouraging when the same thoughts keep repeating themselves despite your attempts at challenging them. This frequently occurs when a person is depressed. Keep trying and don't give up. Soon you will find that you are able to have less of such negative thoughts.

Step 3: Testing Negative Thoughts

This method of testing negative thoughts has been called behavioural experiments. These experiments are meant to challenge the negative thoughts by testing some of the alternative thinking that was created from answering the thoughts. Let us take the example of the teenager who feels that his classmates hate him. The teenager feels that no one is his friend. He can test the validity of that thought by approaching a friendly classmate and striking up a conversation. In his low mood, this can be daunting, but he can practise in his mind how to approach the classmate and what to say.

Do note that behavioural experiments are best done with a supporter (such as the school counsellor). The supporter will be able to provide guidance and prod you to keep trying when you fail the first few times.

04 SUICIDE PREVENTION FOR TEACHERS AND COUNSELLORS

Learning Points

- Suicide in schools is preventable
- Teachers can play a role in the detection and assessment of suicidal youths
- Suicide prevention is the responsibility of everyone and not just the school counsellor or mental health professionals

Although up to 38% of children and adolescents surveyed in overseas studies reported suicidal tendencies[1, 2], only a small percentage of young people actually commit suicide. Nevertheless, the death of a young person by suicide causes immeasurable pain and suffering to family, friends, teachers and classmates and can lead to them experiencing emotional and psychological problems as well[3].

Suicide is not inevitable and can be prevented. Experts suggest that the key thrusts for the prevention of suicide are[4]:

- To build high self-esteem and social "connectedness" within the individual and community which involves developing close ties with family and friends, social support networks, stable relationships, and religious or spiritual commitment;
- To facilitate the early identification and appropriate treatment of mental disorders, especially depression, alcohol and substance abuse;
- To educate primary health care personnel in the identification and treatment of people with mood disorders;
- To develop interventions based on the principle of connectedness and easy access to help such as crisis helplines and on-site counselling facilities;

- To develop psychosocial interventions, suicide prevention centres and school-based prevention centres involving crisis management, self-esteem enhancement and the development of coping skills and healthy decision making; and
- To restrict access to common methods of suicides.

In order for suicide prevention efforts to be effective, there has to be a comprehensive effort made by all sectors of society, including the government, healthcare agencies, schools, law enforcement agencies, religious institutions and the media. Although medical and mental health professionals play a crucial role in risk assessment, the provision of emergency services and treatments, and the development of a knowledge base through research and the evaluation of suicide preventive measures, members of the community have a part to play to reduce the incidence of suicide. The need to openly address the issue of suicide is important as there is a basic lack of awareness about suicide, in part due to the cultural taboos surrounding the subject[5,6].

Importance of School-based Prevention Efforts

Schools are important settings for crisis intervention and grief work as children and adolescents spend a large proportion of their time in schools[7]. In addition, as the goal of schools is to develop the individual not just academically, but also in terms of life skills, schools are the ideal facility through which prevention, intervention and postvention programmes to deal with death and grief issues can be provided for children and adolescents.

In the United States, 25% of secondary schools have suicide prevention programmes[8]. The goals of these programmes include increasing awareness of the problem, identifying teenagers at risk of suicide, providing information about mental health resources and equipping staff and students with coping skills[9]. A comprehensive school-based suicide prevention programme targets the promotion of positive mental health among the staff and students, as well as the education of staff, students and parents about suicide[10, 11].

Studies in the US suggest that youth suicide rates were reduced in counties in which suicide prevention programmes were implemented, while rates for the state during the same period did not decline[12]. There are many counties in each of the 50 states that make up the US. Although some professionals are concerned that discussions on suicide may somehow plant the idea of suicide in young people, the Centre for Disease Control and Prevention in the US states that "there is no evidence for increased suicidal ideation or behaviour following these programs". Experts do caution though that some students may react negatively to these programmes and school personnel have to be prepared to assist any student who finds the programme upsetting. Researchers recommend that suicide prevention programmes should be incorporated into existing health curricula rather than stand alone as a highly visible special programme[13] and some states in the US require parental permission for students to attend such programmes[14].

Role of Teachers and Counsellors[14,15]

The role of the school with respect to suicide prevention and intervention is to:
1. Detect suicidal students
2. Assess the severity level of the suicidal risk
3. Notify the parents of the suicidal student
4. Work with the parents to obtain the necessary mental health services and supervision for the student
5. Monitor the student in school and provide continued assistance to the parents and student

Our local schools should be prepared to deal with youth suicide. This includes not only the primary and secondary school population, but also tertiary institutions. This is especially so as overseas studies have found a suicide rate double that of teenagers among the 20 to 24-year-old population[14].

The Ministry of Education has clearly written and disseminated policies and procedures to clarify the role of school personnel when responding to at-risk students, suicide attempts and completed suicides. School personnel are also given formal training in suicide prevention. These programmes have been incorporated into existing crisis response procedures and health education programmes where appropriate. It is also important to develop links and good working relationships with community agencies that target suicide prevention. Schools need to have in place a list of resources to assist suicidal students. If teachers are unclear about these procedures, it is important that they speak with their school management teams and consult the Ministry of Education's Guidance Branch when in doubt.

While the school counsellor or personnel designated to care for the suicidal student should continue to support and monitor the student in school, the primary person responsible for treating a suicidal student should be a mental health professional specially trained in this area. A co-operative relationship between schools, parents and community mental health services should be established so that suicidal students can be given maximum support and interventions can be quickly put in place should a crisis situation occur.

Finally, there should be a focus on reducing access to means of suicide, and mental health professionals should be engaged to evaluate the programmes for their effectiveness. A school-based suicide prevention programme requires teamwork that includes teachers, school personnel, school nurses, school psychologists and school counsellors working in close cooperation with community agencies. In many societies, some school personnel are not receptive to suicide programmes in schools. This is not surprising as there is a cultural taboo against acknowledging and discussing suicide. Some school personnel are afraid to deal with youth suicide and are reluctant to face the possibility that such an event may happen in their school. Some also believe misconceptions about youth suicide and the myth that talking about suicide will prompt suicidal behaviour. School administrators may also be reluctant to commit limited resources to a problem which tends to be seen as the purview and responsibility of mental health professionals.

PROGRAMMES FOR STUDENTS

There are two approaches to suicide prevention efforts targeted at students. The first focuses on developing the overall mental health and well-being of students through the teaching of coping skills as well as the development of a positive school climate that affirms life and is conducive to the promotion of good mental health among the students[16]. The second approach addresses the issue of suicide with the aims of teaching the students how to identify their friends or peers who are at risk of suicide as well as how and where to get help These presentations inform students about the facts and myths of suicide, the warning signs of suicide, how to befriend a suicidal peer, how to intervene in the event of a suicide crisis, the situational nature of suicide and the community resources available to help suicidal youth[17].

The Positive Mental Health Approach[18]

The positive mental health approach which focuses on developing the overall mental health and well-being of students is recommended by all experts and is in line with studies suggesting that factors such as high self-esteem and being socially well connected and supported are protective against suicide[4].

Strengthening self-esteem in youth[19]

Studies find that positive self-esteem protects children and adolescents against mental distress and despondency, and gives them the resilience to cope better with difficult and stressful life situations[20]. Positive self-esteem in children and adolescents can be achieved through the following approaches:

- Encouraging parents and teachers to accept the child as he is and thus reducing the pressure to do better.
- Encouraging parents to convey love and affection towards their children.
- Providing children and adolescents with positive life experiences that will help to develop a positive self identity[21] and increase their self-confidence in the face of future obstacles.
- Imbuing the child with a sense of mastery and autonomy through the development of physical, social and vocational skills.

Promoting emotional expression[18]

Children and adolescents should be taught to be aware of their feelings and to take their own feelings seriously. They should be encouraged to confide in parents and other adults, such as teachers, school doctors or nurses, friends, sport coaches and religious advisers.

Improving the school environment

Being in a safe, positive and nurturing environment is essential to a child's development and growth. Teachers should be trained to build rapport with their students and to communicate in positive ways. They should identify and support students with difficulties, be it in their school work, family and social relationships or emotional growth. Schools should develop a zero tolerance policy on bullying and violence, and students and staff should be educated on ways to prevent bullying and violence in and around the school premises in order to create a safe learning environment[18].

Availability and access to help and support[18]

Easy access to help should be ensured by having an on-site school counsellor who is available and approachable, and by widely publicising the telephone numbers of crisis and emergency helplines and psychiatric emergency numbers. Students with psychiatric disorders or who misuse drugs or alcohol should be promptly referred for help.

SUICIDE PREVENTION PROGRAMMES

The most important aspect of any suicide prevention programme is the early recognition of children and adolescents in distress and/or at increased risk of suicide[22]. It is a common frustration for mental health professionals that friends often knew about the suicidal actions of the deceased but did not look to adults for help. It is therefore important not just to target students at risk for suicide, but also reach the non-suicidal peer who may be the first to identify that his friend or schoolmate is considering suicide. Thus programmes targeting students are developed in response to the following findings[11]:

- Suicidal youth are more likely to confide in peers rather than adults[23].
- Disturbed youths such as those who are depressed or who are substance abusers prefer peer support over adults.
- Some adolescents, especially males, do not respond to troubled peers in empathic or helpful way.

- Only about 25 % of peer confidants tell an adult about their troubled or suicidal peer.
- School personnel are among the last choices of adolescents for discussing personal concerns.
- Contact with helpful adults is a protective factor for troubled youths.
- Young people who help others, benefit from participating in such interactions as they shape pro-social behaviours and reduce problematic behaviour related to social competencies that carry over to other challenging situations.
- A large number of students hold inaccurate or undesirable views of suicide[24].

It should be pointed out that while all professionals agree that the positive mental health approach is important, opinions differ with respect to the benefits of directly discussing the issue of suicide with students. Some professionals are concerned that classroom presentations on suicide may plant the idea of suicide, while others suggest that such presentations may have adverse effects on students who have suicidal ideation or who have previously attempted suicide. A national survey in the US found that compared to suicide attempters who did not attend any suicide-prevention programme, suicide attempters who participated in the programme were less likely to believe that a mental health professional could help them, were less likely to tell someone about their suicidal thoughts/intentions, and were more likely to view suicide as a reasonable solution[25]. Dr Shaffer, a child psychiatrist, also found that after participating in a suicide-prevention programme, those who had previously attempted suicide were more likely to continue feeling that suicide is a possible solution for problems and that it is a good idea to keep depressed feelings to oneself, as compared to those who had not attempted suicide[26].

However, other professionals argue that when the presentations were carefully designed and presented, participants were found to have (i) short-term increases in knowledge about suicide prevention and the mental health community resources that they could turn to for help and (ii) did not show an increase in suicidal thought and behaviour[27]. Experts emphasise that it is important not to normalise suicidal behaviour by portraying suicide as a "normal" or common response to stress or pressures that could happen to anyone rather than a consequence of a mental illness[25, 28]. Research has indicated that suicide is typically associated with emotional disturbance[29]. Dr Cliffone found that when suicide is portrayed as a "maladaptive act of poor judgement", there was a more positive effect on teenagers who had undesirable attitudes towards suicide before participating in the programme. It also increased the number of teenagers who would refuse to keep a friend's suicidal intentions secret and increased their willingness to refer the friend to a counsellor[24].

Programmes that educate students on suicide prevention typically focus on developing the knowledge, attitudes and skills necessary for responding to at risk peers and obtaining adult help for them. These can be conducted by classroom teachers who have received training in youth suicide prevention and response. Classes could include brief presentations, exercises, videos, roles plays and cover the following areas[10, 25]:

- A discussion of normal adolescent development
- Self-evaluation of emotional well-being
- Facts and misconceptions about suicide
- How to identify a peer at risk of suicide
- How to respond to and help a peer at risk of suicide (for example, knowing the importance of not holding information about suicidal intent in confidence, not attempting to "counsel" suicidal peers, and knowing how to get professional help for a suicidal peer)
- School and community resources available and how to access them
- Provision of wallet cards that contain school and community emergency numbers

PROGRAMMES FOR SCHOOL STAFF

In order to empower school personnel to help a suicidal student, every school should have a clear, written protocol on procedures and staff responsibilities when faced with a suicidal student. School personnel should also receive regular training on the warning signs of suicide, how to respond appropriately and how to obtain help. This enables school personnel to feel better equipped and more confident about helping a suicidal student. Such programmes should involve not only teachers but also teacher aides, canteen operators and school bus drivers[14].

Strengthening the Mental Health of School Teachers and other School Staff[30]

Unless teachers and school staff feel secure and supported in schools, it is difficult for them to respond effectively to suicidal students. It is important to ensure the well-being of teachers and other school staff by making the workplace a safe, supportive and accepting place. They should be helped to understand their own stress and be equipped with adequate skills to cope effectively with their problems and even possible mental illness. They should also have access to support and means of alleviating stress at work. Mental distress or illness should be destigmatised so that school staff who need treatment would be more willing and ready to seek help.

Empowering School Staff[14]

Although school counsellors are the ideal personnel to assess the severity level of a suicidal student's behaviour and should be fully trained and equipped to do so, all school personnel need to be empowered to feel that they could respond effectively and save the life of a suicidal student. They should be helped to work through personal issues and perceived inadequacies and be prepared to cope whenever suicidal issues arise. They should be encouraged to reach out to suicidal students by offering outlets of help such as contact emails and telephone helplines. They should be helped to understand the situational nature of youth suicide and the importance of not keeping suicidal behaviour or plans secret.

Improving the Skills of School Staff[18]

Training courses can be conducted to increase the awareness and understanding of suicide risk among teachers and school staff and to improve their ability to build rapport and communicate effectively with distressed and/or suicidal students. School staff should be trained to talk among themselves and with the students about life and death issues. They should also receive training to improve their skills in identifying distress, depression and personality disturbances, as well as recognising early signs of suicide. They should be taught how to inquire directly about suicidal thoughts and plans and to carefully gather information from the student about his suicidal thoughts, plans and behaviour in a calm and matter-of-fact manner. It may be helpful to conduct role plays and rehearse intervening with a suicidal student. Finally, staff should be advised on the resources and support available when faced with a suicidal student.

Training courses could cover the following areas:
- Facts and misconceptions about suicide
- Causes of suicide
- How to identify students at risk of suicide (warning signs)
- Role of staff (supportive initial responses—identify, respond, refer)
- How to assess the severity of the suicide risk
- Steps to take upon encountering a suicidal student (suicide intervention and crisis management procedures)
- Students' views of characteristics of helpful adults and barriers to help-seeking
- How to communicate with a suicidal student
- Who and how to refer a suicidal student for help (school and community resources)
- School policy and procedures
- Legal issues

EDUCATION OF PARENTS[10, 29, 31]

Although it is not the responsibility of schools to educate parents, schools can facilitate this through parent support groups and other agencies that support parents. The objectives of suicide prevention programmes targeting parents include:
- Helping parents to understand the factors that may lead a child or adolescent to attempt or commit suicide, such as low self-esteem, a sense of abandonment or rejection by a significant other and significant stressors like sibling birth or parental divorce.
- Helping parents understand that suicide for a child or adolescent is an attempt to alter an intolerable situation, a cry for help or a means for

gaining attention, love or affection from significant others. It is better that parents do not exasperate their child until professional help is obtained than to have the young person end his life prematurely[32].

- Helping parents to become aware of their child's moods, feelings and attitudes that may indicate that the child is feeling troubled or experiencing a problem.
- Teaching parents to talk and listen to their child without judgment, criticism or downplaying his feelings and problems.
- Advising parents to seek professional help if the child has serious thoughts about suicide and to consider hospitalisation if necessary.
- Advising parents to remove access to any means of suicide.
- Advising parents on the importance of continuing to support and care for the child after the crisis is over and to follow up with a mental health agency to resolve the issues that resulted in the suicidal thoughts and behaviour.

Education workshops for parents could include:
- Facts and misconceptions about suicide
- Risk factors of suicide
- How to identify if your child is at risk of suicide
- How to assess the severity of the suicide risk
- How to communicate with your child if he is suicidal
- Who and where to go for help
- An overview of the school's suicide response plan
- Restriction of access to means to suicide
- Positive strategies for parenting your teenager

SUICIDE INTERVENTION
When a suicide risk is identified[14, 18], the five main areas of concern are:
1. Communicating with the student and assessment of risk
2. Increased supervision of the student
3. Removal of access to means of suicide
4. Notification of parents
5. Referral to a professional

Communicating with the Student and Assessing the Level of Risk [14,18]

The first step when faced with a distressed and/or suicidal young person is to establish a dialogue and develop a relationship that involves mutual trust and understanding. It is not easy communicating with distressed and/or suicidal children or adolescents as they are often hypersensitive to other people's communication styles. This is because they have often been hurt, disappointed, rejected or disrespected in their relationships and lack trust in others. In addition, they may be ambivalent about whether to live or die, and whether to accept or reject help. They may express this ambivalence and lack of trust through their avoidance of adults and reluctance to speak to them.

The fears and anxieties of the adult may also surface during the interaction and may affect the communication between the adult and the suicidal youth. In some cases, the adult is afraid that asking about the young person's suicidal thoughts and plans may incite the young person into committing a suicidal act. In other cases, the adult has unresolved emotional problems that may surface when he or she encounters a suicidal student. Both the above scenarios may result in communication that is tense and devoid of meaningful exchange. At times, the adult's discomfort may be so great that it may result in an inappropriate response such as verbal or nonverbal aggression. This could aggravate the critical situation.

Experts recommend that a school personnel trained to assess the severity of the suicidal risk, ideally the full time school counsellor, should interview the student and gather careful and thorough information about his case history and his suicidal thoughts and plans in a calm, direct and matter-of-fact manner[33, 34].

While it is important to build rapport with the distressed and/or suicidal student, school personnel and staff members must be reminded of their legal and professional responsibility not to honour confidentiality in situations where the student could be at risk of harming himself. Under no circumstances should a suicidal plan be kept secret.

- Recent suicide attempts
- More than one suicide attempt
- Friend or family member who has committed suicide
- Recent losses in the home or in other social situations
- Prior traumatic event such as sexual abuse
- Isolation or withdrawal from school and friends
- Drug or alcohol abuse including inhalant abuse
- Anti-social behaviour and trouble with the law
- Mental health disorders such as depression and/or schizophrenia
- Difficult social circumstances, especially family problems

Increased Supervision of the Student[29]

A student who has made even mild or indirect suicide threats should be supervised constantly until a trained staff or professional is available to determine the severity of the suicide risk. He should not be allowed to leave the school premises and should be taken to a prearranged room that is safe and non-threatening where he can be supervised. After the suicide risk has been assessed, provisions should be made to ensure that the student will continue to be supervised and monitored by his parents or guardian and that mental health services will be obtained for him. The school personnel or counsellor designated to care for the student should continue to monitor and support the student in school.

Removal of Access to Possible Means of Suicide[18]

It is important to remove or lock up dangerous medicines, pesticides, knives and any other dangerous implements in schools. This can be an important life-saving measure in addition to ongoing psychological support.

Notification of Parents[14, 29]

It is important to notify parents any time it is believed that a student is suicidal. This is so that parents can monitor and supervise their child as well as to ensure that the school has done its part in safeguarding the student's welfare and is not liable should any suicide attempt occur. Even if the student denies making suicidal statements or plays them down, his parents can be informed about what he said or did that caused concern as well as his denial or explanation of his behaviour.

Parents who are informed that their child is thinking of suicide react in different ways ranging from hurt to co-operation to denial and anger. Parents should be advised to be patient, to show care and concern for what their child needs, to take the threats and gestures seriously and to keep an open channel for communication. They should also be advised to obtain the necessary mental health services for their child. It is important to keep a positive note when speaking to parents and to empower them with the belief that their child can be helped. A parent who refuses to obtain professional help for his child should be advised that it is neglectful to do so and that child welfare services may have to be called in. It is recommended that careful records of interactions with suicidal students are kept and that parent notification is documented. It is also advisable to have at least two school personnel present at the conference where parents are notified and for parents to sign a form acknowledging that they have been notified that their child is thought to be suicidal.

Referral to a Professional[14, 18]

When the suicide risk is assessed to be serious, the suicidal young person should be taken promptly and decisively to a general practitioner, a child psychiatrist or an emergency department. Ideally, distressed and/or suicidal students should be brought to the healthcare professional with family members or, if unavailable, personally by a member of the school staff, as this ensures that the young person does not default his appointment at the clinic or hospital, which might happen if the student is referred by correspondence alone. To be effective, the distressed and/or suicidal youth should be seen by a multidisciplinary team comprising doctors, nurses, psychologists and social workers within a health service that is viewed as accessible, approachable and non-stigmatising. In Singapore, a pilot programme called Response, Early Intervention and Assessment in Community Mental Health (REACH) has been started which will be available to all schools by 2012.

The following procedures are recommended when a suicide risk is identified[14, 29]:

1. Stay calm and obtain help from a colleague as soon as possible

Do not become emotional or act shocked.

2. Talk to the student calmly and gather information about his thoughts and plans in a matter-of-fact manner

Ask specific questions about what the student intends to do and when he intends to do it. Find out when he started having thoughts of suicide and how often he has these suicidal thoughts.

3. All teachers, staff members, school counsellors or other school personnel must not under any condition agree to keep a student's suicidal intentions a secret

Under no circumstances should a suicide plan be kept secret. School personnel and staff members should be advised on their legal and professional responsibility not to honour confidentiality in such situations where the student could be at risk of harming himself. The school personnel should explain to the student that he has an ethical responsibility to inform the student's parents.

4. If the means of the threatened suicide is present, determine if the student can be persuaded to relinquish the item/items voluntarily

Where possible, the student should be persuaded to relinquish the means of the threatened suicide. However, school staff or personnel should not use force to remove the item/items. If the student cannot be persuaded to relinquish the means, the police should be called in immediately.

5. Take the suicidal student to a pre-arranged room

There should be a room or area designated for such emergency situations where the student can be taken. It should be designed to be safe, non-threatening and preferably away from the hub of activities in the school. Care should be taken to ensure that there are no objects within the room with the potential to cause harm and other students should be advised to stay away. There should also be another adult and a telephone close by. Once a suicide threat is made, the suicidal student should be taken there as soon as possible.

6. Keep a student who has threatened suicide under constant observation

Even when a threat is mild or indirect, a school personnel should stay with the student constantly until a trained staff or professional is available to determine the severity of the suicide risk. Although this may mean that time and effort may be spent on students who are not truly suicidal, it is better to err on the side of caution.

7. Do not allow a suicidal student to leave the school premises alone

A student who has threatened suicide should not be allowed to leave the school until a trained professional has assessed the level of suicide risk and provisions are made to ensure that the student will be properly supervised and monitored after leaving the school. This should be done even if the threat is mild or indirect.

8. Get the student to sign a no-suicide contract

No-suicide contracts have been found to be effective in preventing suicides. It helps the student take control of his impulses and reduces the anxiety of both the student and the school[35]. If the student refuses, his parents should be informed when they arrive and serious consideration should be given to hospitalising the student. The student should also be provided with the phone numbers of the school psychologist or counsellor as well as the local crisis hotline.

9. Notify the school counsellor or member of staff that has been appointed to receive and act on all reports from various persons about the suicidal student

There will be one or two key personnel whom other teachers or staff should report to about students who are suicidal[35]. The person(s) should be trained in the management of crisis or emergency situations and will act on the reports. The Ministry of Education's Guidance Branch will also need to be informed. Guidelines for this will be available with the school senior management.

10. Inform the suicidal student that outside help has been sought and explain what the next steps will be

Let the student know that help has been obtained and that the professional will assist him in finding help to deal with suicidal thoughts and impulses. Inform the student that his parents or guardians will be contacted and notified of the situation. If the student is resistant to having his family informed, it is appropriate to discuss and convey understanding of his concerns while maintaining the position that suicidal plans and intentions cannot be kept in confidence.

11. Supervise the student until his parents have taken over responsibility

The student has to be kept under constant supervision until his parents have arrived and assumed responsibility for monitoring him and ensuring that mental health services will be obtained for him.

SUICIDE POSTVENTION

Suicide postvention involves efforts to address the effects of a person's suicide, whether attempted or committed, on his friends, family and the individuals around him[29]. This includes the provision of information about the normal reactions following a suicide, therapeutic assistance and support to prevent grief complications and enabling the child or adolescent to achieve psychological healing and readjustment to healthy living[36-39]. A second goal is to reduce the chances of a second suicide as the suicide of a student triples the risk that another suicide will occur[37-40]. This is because distressed children and adolescents have a tendency to identify with those who have attempted or committed suicide and to emulate their destructive approach to solving problems. This does not only include the children or adolescents who knew the suicide victim, but also those who have not known the suicide victim personally or who have never interacted with him.

Students at risk of committing suicide need to be identified and given assistance[29]. School staff and personnel need to be made aware of the warning signs of suicide and given a clear protocol to follow to prevent further suicides. Experts emphasise that a series of planned steps must take place in order to minimise the chance of second suicide and to help students and staff deal with their grief[37–39]. Schools therefore need to have in place emergency plans on how to inform school staff, students and parents, when a suicide has been attempted or committed at school.

The following procedures are recommended when a suicide has been committed[29]:

1. Contact the parents of the deceased

The parents should be contacted directly to verify facts and to express sympathy for their loss. If appropriate, information regarding community resources that the parents could approach should be made available to them[35].

2. Assess the impact on the school

Schools need to assess the number of students affected by the suicide and determine the level of resources required to cope with the impact of the death. Issues to consider when assessing the impact of suicide on the school include the popularity of the person who committed suicide, the number of staff or students who were exposed to or involved in the suicide, whether other suicides had happened in the school in the past and how recently, whether the suicide occurred during a vacation or while school was in session, as well as the level of personal, family, school and community resources available to the school population.

3. Inform the relevant authorities and other institutions/agencies that may be affected

These may include the Ministry of Education as well as other schools which may be attended by siblings or friends of the deceased.

4. Determine what information is to be shared

When a death has occurred, it is important that accurate information is given to the staff and student body in a timely manner. Before the death has been formally classified a suicide, it should be announced simply that a death has occurred. As more information becomes available, the school authorities should determine what information should be shared. This will involve consulting the parents of the deceased for their preferences and their wishes should be respected[41]. They may wish to keep the name of the deceased or specific details of the death confidential. Discretion has to be exercised with respect to the information shared with students. It is important to avoid providing information that may be seen as glorifying the suicide[35] or providing details of the suicide that may be imitated. Information about normal or common responses to a suicide can be provided. In the event that there is absolutely no possibility that students can become aware that a suicide has occurred, it is not necessary to report the death as such or to provide crisis intervention services. This would reduce the emotional and psychological impact of the death on the students. However, if there is any chance that students could come to know of the suicide, it is better for the school to acknowledge the incident than to deny its occurrence[42].

5. Determine how the information is to be shared

Not all students in the school need to be informed about the suicide [35]. Determine the appropriate groups and this should be done in classes or groups where a teacher or staff member can be on hand to directly address the concerns and reactions of the students[42], rather than in an assembly or over a public address system. For students who are considered vulnerable perhaps because of their personal histories or because they were close to the deceased, it may be appropriate to share the information with them either individually or in small groups.

6. Identify high-risk students and plan interventions

High-risk students should be identified and given intervention as soon as possible. Intervention may involve individual or group counselling, classroom activities or presentations, parent meetings, staff meetings and referrals to community agencies. The main objectives of intervention include ensuring that students do not identify with the deceased, do not glorify or romanticise the person's behaviour or circumstances and do not dwell on real or imagined guilt[35]. Students should be helped to express their feelings about the suicide and be assured that it is normal to feel a mix of emotions like sadness, fear, anger and confusion. They should be helped to understand that the suicide is a permanent and irreversible solution to temporary problems and that suicide is a poor choice to make[42]. They should also be helped to see that even though it is not uncommon to experience suicidal thoughts following a suicide[43], they are different from the person who committed suicide[42] and can choose to do things differently.

7. Inform the staff

A staff meeting should be held as soon as possible after the suicide[44, 45] with the purpose of informing the staff on how they can help students cope with the loss and to help staff members deal with their own feelings and responses to the suicide[38]. Staff should be given the facts regarding the death, informed of plans for the provision of crisis counselling services and reminded of the procedures and guidelines for action during a crisis[41, 46]. They should be alerted to the types of students who may be vulnerable or at risk for an imitative response to the suicide and given information on how to make referrals[44]. Staff members who feel personally uncomfortable discussing the suicide with the students should be allowed to express this concern freely and given alternative opportunities for helping in the crisis.

8. Conduct a debriefing

Debriefings should be conducted at intervals after the initial staff meeting to evaluate the intervention process, update on the status of referrals, discuss prioritisation of needs and plans for follow-up actions, as well as to assess how staff members are coping. Debriefings can be helpful in providing mutual support among staff and allowing them to deal with their own feelings and emotions[44, 46].

9. Consider the liabilities of a memorial

Following a suicide, care has to be taken to ensure that the actions of the school do not mystify, glorify or romanticise the suicide. While affected students can be allowed to attend the wake/funeral, it is not advisable to make special arrangements or stop classes in order for students to attend the wake/funeral. It is not advisable to put up plaques, dedications or conduct large-scale assemblies or observances in school to remember the suicide victim as these may reinforce the message that death is a way to gain recognition and attention[47].

10. Provide individual and group counselling

Counselling of affected students should be done individually or in small groups rather than in an assembly. Students should be given the opportunity to ask questions and express their emotions. Emphasise that no one is to be blamed for the suicide, that help is available, that suicide is preventable and that everyone has a part to play in preventing suicides.

Learning Points

- Understanding what depression is
- Knowing that suicide is a permanent solution to a temporary problem

See You Tomorrow

"See you tomorrow!" I could see myself smiling and waving at them from the school gate. A perfect picture. My jaws ached from smiling so hard. The bus smelt like puke but at least I managed to get a seat. I stuffed myself in the corner, away from the pushing, shoving crowd. I felt like choking from the noise, the heat and the smells and there was this drumming in my head that really hurt. It was a good day.

Mrs Lim was in a good mood today. She wasn't screaming at us as much as usual. It's not that I get scolded much. I generally do my work and I'm an average student. But I just can't take the noise when she goes crazy. I get so messed up inside. My heart beats really fast and I have to hold my pencil really tightly to steady the spinning. Nobody knows this about me. Anna and Si Rui are supposed to be my best friends since Secondary One. We go for recess together, hang out in the malls and share a cig now and then. But I don't tell them about my problems and how I feel. Actually I don't know if I really like them. Anna can be quite a b***h sometimes and Si Rui is very competitive. She's always looking at my notes and asking me for my grades. Maybe that makes me a two-faced liar. Pretending to be best friends with people I don't really like. But then I don't really like myself either.

"Hi mum." I'm back home. As usual, she barely looks up from her papers, just goes "em" at me. I used to tell her about my day, until I realised that she wasn't really listening. That's the problem when you get older. You start to notice things you didn't used to. Like the "Hurry up, I've got something I need to do" look or the "I'm so tired and she's just rambling on and on" look. It didn't help that she would turn things I said against me and start lecturing me about them. Obviously, she doesn't know about my smoking. All hell would break loose. I know smoking is bad. Who doesn't? But I can't cope without it. It's not like I'm addicted. It's just so hard living in the first place.

"How did you do in your Maths paper?" She finally finished reading. "Oh okay. 72." "Is that good? How did your other friends do?" "I don't know." "What do you mean you don't know. Don't you ask?" "No." "So are you above average? Or average? Doesn't your teacher tell you?" "I really don't know Mum." "Everything you don't know. I'm just concerned about you okay? If you don't like me asking, then I won't ask anymore!" Great. Now I've pissed her off. She's going to give me the silent treatment for the rest of the day. Like I've done her some great wrong. Not appreciating her caring. I go to my room. I'm not allowed to close the door. "Don't treat your home like a hotel okay?" I feel so tired. There's this tight feeling around my chest, like someone grabbed my heart and squeezed it and won't let go. I can feel my stomach cramping up so I curl up in my bed and wait for it to go away. I used to cry but I don't anymore. Everything's dried up and my mouth aches. I don't have the energy to fight anymore.

My dad's back. I can hear my mum complaining to him about me. He comes to the door. "Jun, why can't you just answer your mother when she talks to you?" He looks so tired. I can see the lines on his face, the gray hairs shouting out his age, telling of his struggles in this wearisome world. I love my dad so much. "I did answer her Dad." In the past, I tried to explain to my dad about my mum. I tried to tell him how hurt I felt when she ignored me, when she acted like I was such a bother, when it seemed like all she cared about were my grades. Even now, I wanted to cry to him about the pain I felt inside, about how much I wanted a cuddle, a touch, to be his little girl again. But I know my dad wouldn't be able handle all this emotion. He would just shut down, turn away, say something like, "Well, your mother cares about you okay? You're just too sensitive."

I don't know what's wrong with me. I have friends, I have parents who love me, I have all the things I want, a good life. People say I am so lucky. I should be so happy. But I feel so empty inside and I just don't seem to enjoy anything anymore. I can laugh and joke when I am with my friends, but at 4 am, I wake up and my pillow is soaked with tears, and I am all alone. Maybe it's me. I'm the one who's lying to others about who I am, pretending to like people that I don't like, hurting the ones that I love. Maybe I'm just no good.

Dear Mum & Dad,

I am so sorry. I love you both very much and the last thing I want is to hurt either of you. But it's just too difficult carrying on like this. It's nobody's fault. Maybe I'm just not strong enough for this world. Please forgive me and I really do appreciate everything that you have done for me.

Your loving daughter,
Jun

When Jun's body was found, nobody could understand why it happened. "She was such a good girl," they said, "Always smiling, always ready to help others." "What did she have to be unhappy about?" they asked, "She had everything going for her. She was such a bright student." "So selfish," some said, "look at her parents now, they are in so much pain. She should have thought about them before she killed herself."

Jun is not a real person, but her thoughts, feelings and experiences are based on real people who have made suicide attempts. Like Jun, many teenagers turn to suicide because they feel trapped in a situation in which they feel powerless to control and in which they see no prospect for change or improvement. Suicide at that point in time seems to be the only way out, and the only form of release from the powerful and intense thoughts and feelings that overwhelm them. Some of these feelings may involve hurt, loss, rejection, abandonment and a sense of being unloved or unwanted. Others may feel anger and hatred, and seek to revenge themselves on those who victimised or hurt them. Still others are fearful, anxious, worried or feel insecure about the world around them, about their future or about their relationships with others. Feelings like guilt or disappointment can also be so strong as to cause an individual to consider suicide.

Some individuals are more likely to be at risk for suicide. These include those who have addictive disorders or mental illnesses[1] such as schizophrenia or depression. Depression in particular has been found to increase the risk of a teenager having suicidal thoughts and behaviour[2]. A local study points to an increase in numbers of teenagers being diagnosed with depression as compared to those aged 10 years and under[3]. Jun and those who knew her may not have been aware that she may have been suffering from depression. If they had known, perhaps help could have been sought and a tragedy prevented. Many teenagers who attempted suicide did not really want to die. They were seeking an escape from feelings that they felt were impossible to tolerate, and from problems that they thought were impossible to resolve.

WHAT IS DEPRESSION?

Many people think of depression as feeling sad or "blue", but depression is much more than that. A person who is depressed has a serious condition that results in changes to his body, the way he thinks about things and the way he feels. Depression puts a filter on the person's way of looking at things and distorts a person's thinking. A depressed person tends to see only the negative aspects of a situation and has difficulty seeing the positive aspects. They focus on their failures and disappointments, and downplay their competencies and self-worth. They are unable to consider other alternatives to their problems. This may explain why a person who resorts to suicide believes that ending his life is the only solution to his problem. Although people might tell a depressed person to just "pull himself together" and stop being depressed, it is really not so simple. Depression can result in chemical changes in the brain which often requires treatment to reverse. When teenagers who made suicide attempts were treated for their depression, it is as if the cloud over their thoughts had lifted and they were better able to see and think clearly. They realised that their problems were not necessarily permanent and that suicide is not the only solution to a bad situation. Their mood was also improved and they could feel pleasure, enjoyment and hope again.

How to Know if a Person is Suffering from Depression

It is not always easy to tell if a person is suffering from depression, as many of the changes are inside the person. However, there are also outward signs such as changes in behaviour or appearance. Take a look at the symptoms of depression listed below. If someone you know exhibits several of these symptoms, he may be depressed. It is advisable that you get the person to seek professional help.

SYMPTOMS OF DEPRESSION[4]

Physical

Changes in appetite or weight

Some people with depression lose their appetite and as a consequence, lose weight. Others may eat more to comfort or distract themselves from their feelings.

Changes in sleep patterns

Some people with depression sleep longer than normal, while others find it difficult to fall asleep. Still others find themselves waking up at odd hours in the night and having difficulty falling asleep after that.

Exhaustion and fatigue

People with depression have very low energy. They feel tired and weary, and find it difficult to move about and do even simple and basic tasks. Some stay in bed for a long time each day because they are too depressed to get up and face the day ahead.

Digestive problems

People with depression may feel constipated or have diarrhoea. They may also feel nauseous.

Headaches, backache, chest pain, muscle aches and pain

Our emotions can affect our bodies. Depression can cause our muscles to stiffen up. This can result in aches and pains in various parts of our bodies.

Cognitive

Unable to concentrate and think clearly

People with depression find it difficult to concentrate on their work or studies and make decisions. A child or teenager whose grades are falling may be suffering from depression.

Poor memory

People with depression tend to become forgetful.

Negative view

People with depression tend to see only the negative aspects of a situation. They see themselves, others and the world around them in a negative light.

Focus on faults and failures

People with depression tend to think that their successes are due to circumstance, chance or luck, and that their failures are due to their personal qualities or traits.

Recurring thoughts of death and dying

A depressed person may talk a lot about death and make plans to end his life.

Emotional

Persistent feelings of sadness, irritability or low mood

People with depression report feeling sad and empty for weeks, months or even years. Children or teenagers with depression may become irritable or cry easily. Some children or teenagers may hide their feelings by withdrawing from others.

Feelings of worthlessness and guilt

People with depression say that they are "no good", and feel that they are a burden to others. Some teenagers with low self-esteem may turn to risky sexual behaviour in order to obtain love and approval and to fill the emptiness that they feel inside.

Feelings of helplessness

A depressed person feels powerless to make changes to his life and to the world around him. He says things like, "There is nothing I can do" and "What's the point of trying?"

Loss of hope

A depressed person does not see the possibility of his situation changing for the better. He says things like, "It will never get better" and "There's no way out".

Anxiety

When a person is depressed, things that seem easy to others become a source of stress, tension and worry. A child or teenager with depression may become fearful and panicky.

Behavioural

Restlessness and slowness

Some people with depression become restless and agitated in their behaviour. Children or teenagers who are depressed may become very active, fidgety and reckless. However, others become slower in their movements. Children or teenagers with depression may appear inactive or less playful.

Avoidance and withdrawal

People with depression tend to experience a loss of interest in activities that they previously enjoyed. Children or teenagers with depression may become "bored" and reject activities that they used to like. They may withdraw from family and friends, and spend a great deal of time in their rooms.

Excessive engagement in an activity

A depressed child or teenager may spend a lot of time on a particular activity such as video gaming.

Dependent behaviour

Some children or teenagers become more demanding and want their family members or friends to do more things for them or to accompany them all or most of the time.

Aggressive or risk-taking behaviour

Depressed people are more likely to get into fights or engage in behaviour that could result in harm to themselves. These behaviours may include cutting themselves, substance abuse or driving recklessly.

While depression increases the risk of a teenager thinking about and planning to end his life, it is not always the case that every teenager who attempts suicide has depression. Many of the warning signs that alert us to the possibility that a teenager is considering suicide are similar to the symptoms of depression. However, there are also more specific signs that indicate that the danger of a teenager ending his life is very real and that action should be taken immediately.

WARNING SIGNS OF SUICIDAL BEHAVIOUR[5,6]

Warning signs can be grouped according to the degree of likelihood that the teenager would kill himself. The first group consists of signs that point to a strong risk that the person is very likely to carry out a suicide attempt. When such strong signs are observed, immediate action is required. A parent, teacher or counsellor should be informed immediately. When warning signs in the second group are observed, there should be concern for the teenager's mental well-being and he should be assessed by a mental health professional. However, there may not be an immediate danger of suicide. These warning signs are sometimes cries for help. The teenager may not really want to die and is sending out signals calling for someone to do something to intervene.

High risk, immediate action required

- Talking or writing about death, dying or suicide.
- Making threats to kill or hurt himself by saying things like "I'm not going to be a problem anymore" or "You won't see me anymore".
- Looking for ways to kill himself such as showing an interest in pills or guns.
- Writing farewell notes or saying goodbye.
- Putting his affairs in order by giving away treasured possessions, clearing up his room, returning borrowed items.

Not an emergency, but an adult should be informed and a mental health assessment is needed

- Talking about death.
- Reading, writing and/or creating art work about death.
- An unusual neglect of personal appearance.
- Sudden and marked change in personality or attitude, for example, a good student who suddenly flouts rules blatantly.
- Sudden change in relationships.
- Sudden unexpected happiness after a period of depression (this could indicate that the depressed person has finally made a decision to commit suicide and feels relieved).
- Sudden and dramatic changes in mood, for example, mood swings and emotional outbursts.

- Appearing anxious and agitated.
- More irritable and cries easily.
- Showing anger, rage and seeking revenge.
- Aggressive, violent or rebellious behaviour.
- Acting reckless or engaging in risky activities, for example, walking on high ledges.
- Heavy use of alcohol or drugs.
- Talking about feeling trapped and having no way out of problems.
- Talking about feeling helpless about being able to change things.
- Talking about being a failure or a bad person.
- Talking about not caring about the future and/or not having a reason or purpose for living.
- Rejecting praise or rewards.
- Withdrawing from friends, family and community.
- Showing no interest in the things around him and the activities he used to enjoy.
- Changes in weight and appetite.
- Difficulty sleeping or sleeping more than usual.
- Frequent complaints about physical symptoms such as stomach aches, headaches and fatigue.
- Sudden drop in school attendance.
- Unable to concentrate and think clearly.
- Sudden decline in school results or quality of schoolwork.
- Inability to complete work.

The Golden Dragon

I walked into my room. There it sat amidst the junkyard on my desk, its mouth serenely arched in a half smile, its wings delicately poised above its head, the scales glimmering in the dusky light of my room. I had wanted it all my life. Well, as long as I could remember anyway. It was a glorious golden dragon, just about the size of my palm. I would reach for it and my brother John would spring forward, steal it from my grasp and hold it teasingly above my head. It was given to him by my Nai Nai when he first started school. He had always been her favourite. Even though I was the youngest of the grandchildren, I could never escape the shadow cast by his celestial light. He was the first grandson, born in the year of the dragon, the special one. And he knew more than any of us how to play up to her. "Nai Nai," he would say, "I'm going to be a doctor and take care of you when I grow up." And she would fawn all over him.

"For you" was all it said on the note next to it. I stared at the words and felt my heart drop. I ran out of the room, the note in one hand, the dragon in the other. "Ma! Where's Kor?" My mum, hearing the fear in my voice, ran out of the kitchen. We did not exchange words. She took one look at the items in my hands and the colour drained from her face. Shortly after he entered the Normal Academic stream in Secondary One, my brother changed. He lost his boyish cheerfulness, conversations were reduced to single word exchanges, and he stopped going out with us. He would come home with school reports that read "Can be moody at times", "Needs to be more motivated with his work", and "Tends to keep to himself," when previously they glowed with compliments about what a friendly, hardworking boy he was. Some of the aunties said, "Oh teenagers are like that. Don't worry, he will grow out of it." But it has been more than two years and he seemed to sink further and further into this deep well. He was a handsome boy and used to be conscious about his appearance, but now, looking at him, you would wonder why girls used to smile and stare at him. His room was a terrible mess and my mum would find crumpled bits of unfinished schoolwork stuffed into corners or lying around the floor. One paper she found had a drawing of naked girl kneeling in a pool of blood, her hand limp on a knife that was lodged in her heart. There was a certain surreal beauty about the picture but I felt a chill just looking at it. I didn't know my brother anymore. It was as if the light in him had been snuffed out, leaving a darkness so impenetrable that try as we might, we couldn't reach him.

Air gun practice was the one activity he maintained interest in for some time. But since last month, he had stopped going even for that. His teacher called my mother. "Mrs Lim, are you aware that John has not been coming for practice? Do you know where he is? He has been very defiant lately and has refused to follow our instructions. I noticed he has not been sleeping well and seems to have lost weight. Is something wrong at home?" That last question hit my mum hard. She and my dad had not been getting along well for several years now. They slept in separate rooms and hardly spoke to each other. My mum had been going on about getting a divorce but up to now, they were still together. When my brother came home, she went ballistic on him. He took her assault for a while, then walked into his room, lifted his laptop high above his head and smashed it onto the floor. The sound that came out of his mouth was like the garbled scream of a mangled puppy. After that, he withdrew further and locked himself in his room whenever he was home. We never found out where he went when he wasn't at air gun practice.

"I will call his handphone." The phone rang before my mother could make the call. "Hello Auntie." It was Derrick, my brother's friend from primary school. He was the one person my brother still seemed to maintain some contact with. "I'm worried about John. He called me last night at 2 am. He sounded a bit like his old self again. He was joking around and saying something about having come to terms with being a failure and that it doesn't matter anymore. And that he was going to show those kids in school that he wasn't going to take their bullshit anymore. I thought maybe it's a good thing, that he had come to some kind of realisation or something, but this morning, I had this uncomfortable feeling about him, so I thought I had better call you…" My mother crumpled into a ball on the floor and started shaking and crying. "Call your father!" she sobbed.

The rest of the day was spent making phone calls and driving around looking for John. We peered anxiously at the landings of every HDB flat we passed, hopeful yet fearful of what we might find. The school sent out teams of teachers and students to search the school grounds and the areas surrounding the school. He was nowhere to be found. My father tried calling the police but we were told that we could only file a missing person report after 48 hours. The wait was unbearable. Our hearts would leap whenever the phone rang, only to fall once again into the pits of our stomachs.

I lay in bed staring at the ceiling. It was 1 am. My parents and a few of our relatives gathered in the living room. From time to time, I could hear my mother crying hysterically. At one point, she screamed at my dad, blaming him for the years of neglect. I was told to get some rest, but they should know that it was impossible to sleep. My body was wrecked with exhaustion, but my mind could not relax and I was alert to every sound, movement or flicker of light. I thought how crowded the house was and how cold.

A piercing scream rang through the house. I ran out of my room, only to see my mum, her arms wrapped around my brother, weeping profusely, the tears streaming down her face and her body shuddering with the intensity of her sobs. "Ah John!" she cried, "Where were you? I thought you were dead!" My brother had a stricken look on his face. He appeared in shock, as though he had been through the horrors of hell and back. He opened his mouth and tried to answer, but nothing came out. He appeared choked up and his arms flailed weakly by his side. Then, as though the life had finally been drained out of him, he allowed himself to fall into my mother's arms, curled up there like a baby and wept.

THINK ABOUT

1. Did John try to kill himself? What makes you think so?
2. Why did he contemplate taking his own life?
3. Read through the story again and pick out the warning signs that should have alerted his family and friends that he was at risk for suicide.

WHAT CAN I DO?[7–10]

If you are feeling troubled or depressed, here are some tips on how you can help yourself.

1. Go to someone you trust to talk to about how you feel

You are not alone with your problems. Choose someone whom you feel you can talk to. It may be a friend, teacher, a relative or the school counsellor. We do not need to solve our problems by ourselves all the time. Sometimes we can do with some help.

2. Pick a good time and place to talk

Approach the person and tell him that you would like to talk to him about something important. Then make an appointment to meet up. Choose a time and place where you can talk without any distractions or interruptions.

3. Plan what you want to say

Think about what you want to get out of the meeting. Jot down what you want to say so that you will not miss out anything. If you have any ideas about what may help, share them with the person.

4. Listen and allow the person to help

Be open to what the person has to say. Clarify any misunderstanding calmly. It is okay to ask for and to receive help. We do not have to solve all problems on our own or be on top of things all the time.

5. Be around people who are caring and positive

If you are feeling down, being around people who are negative can make you feel worse. Be around people who are positive and caring.

6. Work with a therapist or counsellor if you need to

Sometimes it is not easy to talk to someone who is close to you. It may be easier to talk to an outsider who is neutral and objective, and whom you do not have to be afraid of hurting with the things that you want to say.

IF YOU ARE CONSIDERING SUICIDE

1. Remember that suicide cannot be reversed

Thoughts of suicide are often triggered by a crisis. You are overwhelmed by your problems and cannot see an end to them. However, problems are often resolved over time, and with some help from others. Many teenagers who attempted suicide were glad that they did not die when they realised that their problems could improve and that better feelings and experiences could come their way. When you end your life prematurely, you are not giving yourself that chance to experience a better life.

2. Know that depression is like any other illness and can be treated

When you are depressed, it triggers a chemical imbalance in your brain which causes the depression. Like other illnesses, depression is treatable. With medication and/or therapy, the depression will gradually lessen, and you will able to think and see things more clearly, and eventually feel good again.

3. Talk to someone

Do not keep suicidal thoughts or intentions to yourself. Allow others to help you see things in a different way or help you find solutions to your problems. It is okay to ask for help. You do not have to be alone with your problems.

IF SOMEONE YOU KNOW IS FEELING TROUBLED AND DEPRESSED

1. Show that you care

Often, people who are troubled find themselves withdrawing from others, thinking that they would not understand how they are feeling. If you think someone you know is feeling troubled, approach the person gently by saying something like "I noticed that you haven't been coming out with us much lately. I am concerned about you and how you feel. Is there anything you'd like to talk about?"

2. Listen attentively

For someone who is feeling troubled and alone, just having someone around to listen to their problems without judging them can be very helpful. Repeat what you hear your friend say in your own words so that he knows that you are listening and making an effort to understand him. Ask him if you are hearing him correctly and get him to clarify areas that you are unsure of. Be respectful of his opinions and values. Do not feel the need to offer solutions right away. If you don't know what else to say, a touch of the hand or just being there for your friend can make all the difference.

3. Offer help

Be a source of support for your friend. Be available when he needs to talk. You may also need to encourage him to seek help from an adult, such as a parent, teacher or counsellor. If your friend is depressed, he may not be able to come up with solutions to his problems on his own. Professional help is necessary in such situations. Offer to go with your friend to seek help from an adult. If your friend refuses to talk to an adult and you feel that his condition is serious, you may need to inform an adult about him. People who are severely depressed may not be able to recognise that they need help. Your friend may get angry with you, but you will feel better knowing that your friend is receiving the help he needs.

IF YOU SUSPECT SOMEONE IS CONSIDERING SUICIDE

1. Watch him carefully

Observe your friend's behaviour and be alert to any warning signs that may suggest that he is planning to end his life.

2. Ask about suicide

It may feel awkward and difficult asking if a person is thinking of suicide, but people who are thinking of suicide are often actually relieved to be asked this question. You are not putting ideas in his head, but giving him an opportunity to talk about how he feels. You may want to explain why you are asking, but be direct. For instance, you could say, "You have been saying that you wish you were dead. Are you thinking about ending your life?" Ask him if he has a plan, what he intends to do, when he plans to do it, and whether he has the means by which to carry out his plan.

3. Listen

Pay attention to what your friend has to say, do not interrupt and do not be judgmental. Take whatever he has to say seriously. Stay calm, caring and open to whatever he has to say. Be careful not to act shocked or embarrassed, or to ignore or minimise his problems. Do not criticise or downplay his feelings. Never challenge or dare him to carry out his suicide plans.

4. Get help

Encourage your friend to seek help from an adult. If your friend refuses, don't do nothing. Go on your own to an adult that you trust and obtain his assistance.

5. Never keep suicidal intentions a secret

Even if your friend insists on secrecy, you must never keep information about suicide a secret. Inform a parent, teacher or counsellor, call the police or a crisis hotline. You may save your friend's life and enable him to find answers that he has not been able to identify because of his condition. You will also save yourself a tremendous burden of guilt that you would experience should your friend take his own life. Remember that suicide is an irreversible response to problems that may be temporary. Many teenagers who attempted suicide are glad that they did not die when they realised that there were solutions to their problems.

6. Stay with your friend

If you feel that your friend is close to committing suicide, do not leave him alone. Continue talking to him about his feelings in a non-judgmental way. Call for help and get someone who is trained to deal with crisis situations involved as soon as possible.

7. Remove any possible means of suicide

If you can identify any item that your friend could use to carry out a threatened suicide, try to take the item away from him. This may be medication, a poisonous substance or any sharp object like a blade or knife. However, you should never use force to remove the item from your friend. If you can, get help from an adult. If your friend refuses to relinquish the item voluntarily, you may need to contact the police for help.

TRUE OR FALSE

Read these scenarios and think about whether the last statement is likely to be true or false.

Scenario 1

Susan has always been one of the top students in our class, but since the beginning of this term, she has been failing and not handing in her work. She is also frequently absent from school and has not been hanging out with the rest of us. The other day, she snapped at us and started crying when one of us asked if there was anything troubling her. I think she may need to see someone for help. True or false?

True. Susan is showing signs of emotional distress and has difficulty coping with her school work. She is also withdrawing from her friends. These symptoms suggest that it is possible that she may be depressed. She should see a mental health professional to be properly assessed and treated.

Scenario 2

Yesterday, Hong Boon told me that he was having thoughts of killing himself. He made me promise not to tell anyone and said that if I was his friend, I should respect his wish to end his pain by taking his own life. If I were to break my promise to him, I would not be a true friend to him. True or false?

False. We must never keep a friend's suicidal intentions a secret. No matter how much he begs or threatens you, you must get help as soon as possible. It is better to have him angry with you for betraying his confidence than to have him dead because you kept his secret. You will feel very guilty if he should die as a result of suicide which you could have prevented. Often people who are thinking of suicide have reached a point where they are desperate and cannot see any other way out. Suicide is often an expression of intense emotional distress and despair. Many are not completely sure they want to end their lives and are often glad that they did not die when they realised that things did indeed get better.

Scenario 3

I took a shortcut home the other day and saw Shin sitting under the stairwell of a block of flats. She was cutting her thigh with a penknife. I saw a whole line of raised red scars across her thigh. She threatened me and said that I would be in big trouble if I told on her. She is a mean person and a bully in school. Why should I care if she lived or died. I'm sure I won't feel anything even if she died. True or false?

False. If you knew about someone's problems and did nothing to help, it is very unlikely that you would be unaffected by her death. This is especially so if you witnessed behaviour that involved the person harming herself and said nothing about it. Even if you are not close or don't like her at all, you are still likely to feel guilty should she commit suicide.

Scenario 4

Angie was especially moody in school this morning and Sharon just saw her buying two packs of Panadol from that pharmacy. Angie has been seeing the school counsellor since her father passed away two months ago. She has said a few times that it would have been better if she had died instead of her father. I think we should keep an eye on her and tell an adult about this straightaway. True or false?

True. Here are several warning signs of possible suicide. Angie's father had just passed away. The grief and pain from the loss of a parent can be overwhelming for a young person and can lead to thoughts of suicide. Angie has in fact mentioned wanting to die. She has been seeing a school counsellor which suggests that she is having difficulties coping. Her moodiness and her behaviour of buying an excessive amount of medication suggests that she may be planning to attempt suicide. You should keep a close watch on Angie and inform an adult immediately.

Scenario 5

Ever since Joshua's girlfriend cheated on him, he has not been himself. He has outbursts of anger and behaves recklessly. He has also mentioned that he will make his girlfriend regret what she did to him. I am afraid that he may do something stupid but I dare not ask him because I don't want to put the idea in his head. True or false?

False. If a person has no intention of killing himself, talking about suicide will not make him want to do it. However, if a person is already thinking about ending his life, asking him about it will open up an avenue for him to talk about his feelings and his problems. After talking through his problems, he may feel supported and find other solutions to his problems. This may lessen his sense of hopelessness and wanting to die. If he cannot be deterred from his suicide plans, knowing his intent allows you to take decisive action to stop him by informing an adult or someone who can help.

Scenario 6

I can't believe Brandon attempted suicide. He is always so cheerful and charming, and really well-liked. Only depressed people commit suicide. True or false?

False. Although depressed individuals are at higher risk for suicidal thinking and behaviour, it is not only those who are depressed who attempt suicide[11]. Suicide is not restricted to one particular personality type or condition. Any type of person can be at risk for suicide. Sometimes, a person attempts suicide out of impulse, after a desperately upsetting situation such a breakup or a bad fight with a parent. For others, their outward appearance of cheerfulness and apparent well-being may mask their inner turmoil. While a person's suicide attempt may be unexpected, we should always be alert to the possibility that even those who appear cheerful, calm or well-adjusted on the outside may be at risk for suicide.

Scenario 7

Teck has just been caught for taking drugs. He is in big trouble now. Poor guy! He has so many problems. His parents are divorced, he is failing in school and his girlfriend just left him. With problems like that, it is better to die and end it all. True or false?

False. Suicide is never a good choice for solving problems. No matter how bad things get, there is always a chance that they will get better. Problems may resolve or improve over time, but ending your life is permanent and irreversible. The person who has committed suicide does not give himself a chance to experience the possibility of a better life in the future. If he is doing it in order to express anger or exact revenge, he will not be around to witness the effects of his suicide.

Cop Blames Himself

In 2008, a police officer found a secondary school student sleeping at the void deck of a block of flats. After checking her identity card, he realised she was wanted for a case of shoplifting. On the day that she was to be charged for her offence, she was found dead at the foot of an HDB block of flats. After this incident, the police officer wrote in his blog, "I am a murderer. If only I did not screen her on that day..."[1]

AFTER A SUICIDE

Although he was not a close friend or family member of the girl, the police officer who arrested her for shoplifting was deeply affected by her suicide and blamed himself for her death.

The suicide of a young person is often sudden and unexpected. It is shocking and distressing not just to those who were close to the deceased, but also to members of the community who received news of the death. Those who were in contact with the deceased shortly before the suicide may feel implicated in her death.

Suicide challenges our trust in an orderly and predictable world. It is particularly disturbing because of what it suggests about the deceased's state of mind that resulted in him taking his own life. This, together with the stigma and blame surrounding a suicide, leaves survivors feeling shocked, angry, resentful, guilty, ashamed and confused[2].

Because the suicide of a friend or acquaintance is such a traumatic experience, the feelings and reactions that a surviving peer may experience can be overwhelming. Different people experience different feelings and reactions to the suicide. For some people, there is an immediate reaction. Others may take a longer time to process the event and the reaction is delayed. Still in others, there may be no strong reaction at all. Sometimes, many different emotions can be felt at the same time. A person's experience with death, his religious beliefs, cultural practices as well as his family and community's response to death will all affect how he responds[3]. It is important to know that all feelings and reactions are normal and natural. There is no right or wrong way to feel.

Here are some of the different ways in which the after-effects of a suicide are felt[3, 4]:

Disbelief

"I can't believe she killed herself. Maybe it was an accident. Or maybe it was an impulsive thing. It doesn't seem like something she would do. She had everything going for her, studies, friends. Why would she kill herself?"

Detachment

"I don't know what's wrong with me. When my friend Wendy died, everyone was crying except for me. We were supposed to be close so how come I didn't feel anything? They said her face was pretty smashed up but the undertaker did a good job with the make-up, you couldn't really tell."

Guilt

"I couldn't eat or sleep for weeks after Bee Hoon died. Maybe I could have done something to prevent it. We used to be close, but I don't know, maybe I have been too busy, I didn't notice that he had changed. Or maybe I noticed but didn't really pay attention. I should have done something. If only I had spent more time with him…"

Blaming the Deceased

"He should have thought about his parents, the pain and anguish he caused them. Suicide is a really selfish and irresponsible thing to do. I mean, to kill yourself over something like that? Come on, life's unfair, all right? So deal with it!"

Blaming Others

"It's all Chong Beng's fault! He was always so mean to him. Always teasing and bullying him. I hope he's happy. I hope he can sleep knowing what he's done!"

Anger

"I hate it when they say I know how you feel. I really want to hit them. How can they know how I feel?"

Resentment

"I would cry and scream at the same time. I pounded my pillows, threw things around. It was so unfair. I was the one hurting, and then he had to go kill himself. Why does it always have to be about him?"

"It's been two years since my brother died, and mum still can't move on. It's Christmas, for goodness sake, can't we just be happy for a bit? Hasn't he caused us enough pain already? I just want to get on with my life."

Shame and Embarrassment

"The first day I walked into school after my brother died, I felt that everybody knew and that everyone was looking at me. I could almost hearing them whispering about me, wondering what's wrong with my family, whether I'm also going to kill myself. My classmates spoke to me really carefully, as though I was going to break apart any moment. If they could, they avoided looking at me. I felt like a ghost walking around, like I was there but not really there."

Stigma

"When I mention suicide, they look down, turn away. They don't want to talk about him, and they act like he did not exist. As if that would make it all go away. But he did exist, and I want to talk about him."

Rejection

"It's hard to believe that he really wanted to die. My parents loved him so much, gave him so much. It's hard to accept that all they had done, all the sacrifices they had made, was not enough."

Confusion and Anxiety

"I kept asking why. How could this have happened? I went over it, again and again. I felt so confused and frightened. I was sad, I was angry, I blamed him, I blamed myself. I was terrified that Dad would kill himself too, or Mum, or Adrian…"

Intense Sadness

"For months I cried and cried. Every morning I wake up and I cry. Before I sleep I cry. Getting through each day was just survival. I'd give anything to have her back. How could she do this? How could she leave me with so much pain?"

Relief

"Don't tell anyone about this, but there is a part of me that feels glad that he is gone. I feel so guilty about that, but it has been so long and so hard. We kept bringing him in and out of the hospital and he was in so much pain anyway. He's probably at peace now."

Suicidal Feelings

"I didn't want to go on living. It felt like all the joy had been sucked out and there was no point in going on. He changed my life and now he's gone. There is nothing to live for anymore."

Isolation and Loneliness

"No I'm not in the mood. I don't know how you people can go out and have fun after what has happened. It's only been two months since Ping died. How can you forget so easily?"

AM I NORMAL?

For the family members and friends of someone who died by suicide, the experience can be as traumatic as being involved in an accident or a burglary. Suicide is not something that happens normally. Suicide is deeply shocking and distressing. When faced with the suicide of someone near and dear, the reactions and feelings may be so overwhelming that you are unable to cope with your day-to-day activities. You may feel numb and detached from the rest of the world. You may also find yourself having recurrent nightmares and may experience the event playing over and over again in your mind. This may affect your ability to concentrate and think clearly. You may experience physical reactions such as headaches and fatigue. You may also have sleeping difficulties, experience changes in your appetite, become more withdrawn and may turn to smoking or drinking as a way of coping. Your mood may be affected and you may become more irritable or experience mood swings. These are all normal reactions that a person experiences when he has undergone a traumatic experience[5, 6].

COMMON REACTIONS TO A TRAUMATIC EVENT[5, 6]
Emotional Reactions

- Numbness, shock
- Denial, disbelief
- Stress, anxiety, worry, apprehension, fear
- Confusion
- Anger, resentment
- Irritability, moodiness
- Sadness
- Detachment, estrangement, alienation

- A sense of vulnerability, insecurity
- Feeling overwhelmed and out of control
- Guilt at surviving, for not having done enough

Effects on Thinking

- Inability to concentrate
- Forgetfulness
- Playing the event over and over in your mind
- Recurrent vivid dreams or nightmares about the event
- Feeling or behaving as if the event were occurring all over again
- Forgetting an important aspect of the event
- Being highly alert to your surroundings

Physical Reactions

- Sleeping difficulties
- Changes in appetite
- Fatigue
- Headaches
- Muscle aches

Behavioural Changes

- Withdrawal
- Avoidance of people, places or activities associated with the event
- Over-activity

Many of the above reactions to a traumatic event like suicide are the body's natural way of helping you cope. When you first hear of the suicide of a loved one, your body may respond by shutting down, leaving you feeling numb as if the situation is unreal and not really happening. This is because your mind is giving the body time to slowly absorb the news and respond to the flood of feelings that will come[7].

However, as the experience starts to sink into the awareness and the news becomes more real to you, you may find yourself thinking about it over and over again, having dreams about it, and talking about it. This is the way your mind processes the event and tries to understand and organise the information surrounding the event. At the same time, you might find yourself being overly alert to your surroundings as you try to protect yourself from the dangers in a world that has suddenly become less stable and secure. You may also become over-active as you try to distract yourself and cope with the influx of feelings that you might experience.

Sometimes though, these natural reactions may not be helpful if they are too intense or continue for too long a time. For instance, if the avoidance of places, people and situations associated with the traumatic event is carried on for too long or develops into a phobia, your long-term functioning may be affected. You may also delay and prolong the grieving process by avoiding reminders of the event and not acknowledging and accepting that the event has occurred and that the person you once knew is gone. Numbness and/or over-activity may also be unhelpful if they prevent you from dealing with your feelings in the long run.

WHAT IS GRIEF AND BEREAVEMENT?

Grief is a response to the loss of something important to us[8]. It is not only experienced when someone dies, but can also be experienced when we lose something that means something to us, such as discovering that the person whom we regarded as our best friend has been lying to you all that time. Grief expresses three things:

1. Feelings about the loss, such as shock, disbelief, guilt, disappointment, anger, fear, isolation, loneliness, confusion and helplessness.
2. Protest at the loss, wishing that it was not true and wanting it to be undone.
3. The effects of the loss on the individual[9]. Grief reactions cover a wide range of physical, mental, emotional and spiritual responses.

Bereavement, on the other hand, is a response specific to the loss of someone through death. This includes grief as well as attempts to make meaning from the loss of someone we know[10]. When we say a person is bereaved, we mean that he has lost someone through death. When a person dies, it is normal and natural to experience grief.

Grief responses are very personal and differ from person to person. There is no right or wrong way to grieve, although many people share similar responses to the death of someone they know and some researchers suggest that all grief responses fall into three broad phases. The first phase is avoidance. This is when the person first learns of the death and responds with shock, denial or disbelief. The second phase is confrontation, during which the person realises that the deceased is truly gone from this world and experiences intense emotions. The third phase is reestablishment. During this phase, emotions gradually become less intense and the bereaved starts to be less preoccupied with the death and becomes more engaged socially and emotionally with the everyday world[9]. While people may go through each of the phases in sequence, it is also normal for grieving individuals to move back and forth across the phases.

There is no time limit for grieving. It is a process that could last over weeks, months or even years. For many people, grief over the loss of a loved one is something that remains with them for the rest of their lives. It becomes a part of their lives and changes the way they see and experience themselves, others and the world around them. As the years pass, they continue to re-experience the absence of someone who was once an important part of their lives. Special dates or encountering sights and sounds associated with the deceased may trigger intense feelings months or even years after the death. Feelings of missing the loved person may never completely go away, although they become less intense and easier to cope with in time.

TASKS OF GRIEVING[11]

The goal of grieving is to learn to live with the changes that come with the loss of the significant person. The bereaved has to accomplish four tasks of grieving in order to achieve a healthy adjustment to the loss. These are:

1. Understanding

This task involves recognising that the person is no longer alive and will never be around again. This requires that honest and accurate information is given and accepted as true by the bereaved individual.

2. Experiencing and Expressing Feelings

The bereaved person has to experience and express the feelings that come with the loss. These feelings may include sadness, anger, guilt, distress, loneliness and so on.

3. Remembering

It is important to remember the life of the person who has died. This may be done by looking at pictures, writing about him or talking about who the person was, what he did when he was alive, his relationships and his achievements. By doing so, the focus is taken away from the death itself, while confirming the reality that the person is gone and affirming the value of human life.

4. Moving On

The bereaved person has to go on with the usual activities of living. This may be hard to do initially as he is overwhelmed with the emotions of grief. However, as time passes, the pain becomes less acute and there are longer periods of calm and peace. While the bereaved person does not forget or get over the loss completely, he becomes better able to cope and learns to live with the loss.

A bereaved individual who accomplishes these four tasks of grieving is able to maintain a state of psychological health and would be stronger and better equipped to cope with future losses.

GRIEF AS A RESULT OF SUICIDE

The grief that results from a suicide is a different form of grief that can take far longer to process. Unlike a death from a terminal illness, suicide is unexpected and out of the blue, leaving family members and friends little time to anticipate and prepare themselves for the death[2]. It leaves questions about why the deceased killed himself which often has no clear answers. Family members and friends are often left feeling confused and guilty, wondering if there is something that they could have done to prevent the suicide.

There is also less social support for those who have lost someone to suicide. Because suicide is not sanctioned by society and is considered morally objectionable in some religions, there is stigma attached to the death of someone by suicide[2]. People often react to the news of suicide with shock, shame, embarrassment, discomfort and awkwardness[4]. They are uncertain how to respond to close friends and family members of someone who has died by suicide and may react by distancing themselves from them or avoiding talk of the deceased. It is not uncommon for the survivors to feel lonely and isolated as a result.

GRIEF IN YOUNG PEOPLE

Teenagers are moving towards becoming adults and have the task of figuring out what lies before them in the years ahead. They are in the process of discovering who they are, what they can do and what they will become. For some teenagers, the idea of their own death or the death of family members and friends may be of great concern as they grapple with thoughts about their future and the nature of their existence in this world. For others, death is something that happens to older people and may seem distant and remote.

Young people who are bereaved over a friend's death are often not given appropriate attention as priority and attention is focused on the surviving family members[12]. Thus they often feel isolated and unsupported. Death of a peer challenges the adolescent's sense of himself as indestructible and makes him question his standing in a world that was previously safe and secure[13].

What is a Grieving Teenager Likely to Experience?

For a teenager faced with the death of another young person, important concerns centre around what the death means to him personally and how his response to it will affect the way people view him. Questions that may arise include:

- "How am I personally involved in this death? Did I do anything to contribute to this death? Is there anything I should do to make things better?"

- "What does this mean about my own life and death?"
- "How does this change my goals in life?"
- "How does this affect the way I view or lead my own life?"
- "How does this affect the way I expect people around me to view or lead their lives?"
- "How does this affect my relationships with others?"
- "How does this change my beliefs and values?"
- "What spiritual meaning does this have for me?"
- "Why am I feeling (or not feeling) this way?"
- "Is my reaction normal? How is a person supposed to behave?"
- "What will others think of me if they knew how I am feeling?"
- "What will others think of me if they see me reacting this way?"

Because teenagers are concerned about what others think of them and do not want to be rejected by their peers, they may feel uncomfortable about showing or expressing their thoughts and feelings about the death[14]. They may avoid participating in social activities because they worry about being asked about the death and fear being embarrassed should they lose control of their feelings. They may find it awkward to express condolences and may appear aloof, detached or indifferent. Some teenagers may develop physical complications such as stomach aches, headaches, rashes, and/or bowel or bladder problems. Eating and sleep disturbances may result. The emotional distress experienced by teenagers may also be expressed in the form of behavioural changes, such as a loss of interest in peer activities, staying home to be closer to family members, or becoming more dependent and reliant on family members. There may also be an increase in impulsive, defiant or antisocial behaviours such as stealing, vandalism, use of illicit drugs or alcohol and sexually promiscuous behaviour[15].

For a teenager, there is a clear awareness of the fact that death is final and irreversible, and that it happens to all living things. However, for a teenager, death is not typically expected in the immediate future. The death of a peer raises questions about the possibility of personal death and can generate feelings of anxiety and instability. It is normal for teenagers to respond to these feelings by denying and distancing themselves from the possibility of death in the near future. Another response is to glorify the death and the deceased, which can create an unhealthy preoccupation and fascination with suicide[16].

HOW TO FEEL BETTER AFTER
LOSING SOMEONE TO SUICIDE[5, 17–19]

1. Expect to Feel Lots of Emotions

These emotions include shock, denial, sadness, anger, guilt, shame, loneliness, isolation and confusion[4]. The experience of grief can be overwhelming, even frightening, as you deal with emotions that may be unfamiliar and disorienting. You may even experience strange sensations and feel extremely vulnerable[2]. Many of these feelings are normal. It may help you feel better if you share your thoughts and feelings with someone you trust.

2. Talk About What Happened

Talking about what happened helps you to process the event and make sense of it. Even though it is natural to want to deny that the event occurred, you should resist the urge to shut down and avoid talking about it. The memories and feelings will not just go away, but will stay for some time. It is more helpful to talk about them and to deal with them than to expect to forget about them. Keep in touch with information about the event and any new developments. This helps you to keep the event "real" and enables you to come to terms with what has happened and how it has affected you.

3. Express Your Feelings

Don't keep to yourself and bottle up your feelings. Share them with other people whom you trust and who have had similar experiences. Knowing that other people share similar feelings and responses helps you to feel that you are not alone and that your reactions are normal. You can also express your feelings in other ways such as writing in a journal or creating a piece of artwork.

4. Get Support From Others and Express Your Needs.

Many people who have lost loved ones find comfort in visits and messages from friends and family members. This is a time when you need to feel connected to others. Be around other people who are caring and supportive. Losing someone to suicide can often be a very lonely and isolating experience as many people do not know what to say or how to help. Be honest and take the initiative to let them know what they can do to help you. It is also all right to ask that they leave you alone sometimes and give you space to deal with your own feelings.

5. Know That It Was Not Your Fault

It is normal to feel guilty and to wonder if you have missed something or could have done something to stop the suicide of your friend. It is not always easy to tell when a person is depressed and thinking of suicide. Some individuals are good at hiding their feelings and do not openly exhibit behaviours that alert others to their problems. It is important to know that sometimes there is no warning and you cannot be expected to predict if a person is about to kill himself. Some friends and family members may also blame themselves for not having done enough to help the person with his problems. Very often, a person's suicide stems from a multitude of factors and there is no one clear reason for his decision to die. Even if more could have been done to help the person with his problems, it is important to know that the decision to kill himself was made by the deceased himself and no one else was responsible for that decision. Healing involves forgiving both yourself as well as the person who died.

6. Keep to Your Routine

Even though it may be hard, try to continue to live your life as before. Do the things you used to do before the event occurred such as attending classes or outside school activities. Maintaining a routine can help you to feel more stable and secure.

7. Take Care of Yourself

Grieving is hard work. It is not only emotionally draining, but can also tire you physically. Make sure that you eat well and get enough rest and sleep.

Physical exercise is also helpful because it releases endorphins which will lift your mood.

8. Do Things That You Enjoy

You may feel that it is inappropriate to engage in enjoyable or pleasurable activities when something as upsetting as a death has occurred. However, caring about the person you lost does not mean that you have to be miserable all the time or deny yourself all joy. It is all right to laugh and joke even as you remember the person you lost. Listening to music or doing things that are relaxing and enjoyable will also help to ease feelings of stress and tension.

9. Be Careful

After experiencing a traumatic event, you will feel stressed and on edge. Accidents are more likely to occur when you are in such a state. Avoid higher-risk activities such as trail biking or doing stunts during this time.

10. Support a Friend

Helping and supporting someone else can help you to feel better. You know that you are not alone and are doing your part to help others cope.

11. Do Something Positive to Remember the Person

Having good memories of the person and sharing them with others is a helpful way to come to terms with the loss of someone that meant something to you. You can write a poem, song or letter, attend the wake or funeral service, make a scrapbook, or look at photos with a friend or family member. Do not be afraid to refer to the person by his name or to share stories about his life. By doing so, you direct the focus away from the way the person died to the life of the individual.

12. Expect Some Days to be More Difficult

Certain dates like the person's birthday, holidays or the anniversary of their death will trigger memories of the person and may bring back intense feelings of loss, sadness and anxiety. You may want to find support with friends or family members, talk to someone you trust or simply find time to be alone and to reflect.

13. Talk to a Counsellor or Join a Support Group
You may find it difficult to speak to close friends or family members about deeply personal matters. If so, you can contact a counsellor or therapist who is professionally trained to help young people deal with emotional issues. You can also call a youth hotline to talk about your feelings or join a support group where you will meet people who are in the same situation as you.

HOW CAN I HELP MY FRIEND WHO HAS LOST A LOVED ONE TO SUICIDE?[18–20]

1. Learn About the Grief Process
Find out about what a person goes through when bereaved and what the normal grief responses involve. This is so that you can assure your friend that her reactions are normal and also help to identify if and when your friend may need additional help.

2. Express Concern and Be There For Your Friend
People who are grieving may feel alone and often find comfort in visits and messages from friends and family members. You do not need to say too much. Often just your presence alone can be very helpful to a friend who is grieving.

3. Give Time For Your Friend to React to the News
It is normal for a bereaved person to take some time to absorb the news of the death. Suicide is often unexpected and people tend to respond with disbelief. Sometimes, there may even be little or no response. Numbness and denial of what happened may be your friend's way of taking in the shock gradually, so that she is not overwhelmed by the intense emotions all at once.

4. Acknowledge the Loss

Let your friend know that you recognise that your friend has lost someone who meant something to her. Do not minimise the loss.

5. Do Not Be Afraid to Talk About the Deceased

Talking about the deceased helps your friend to process the death and her feelings and responses. Do not be afraid to refer to the deceased by name or to share stories and memories about the person. Remembering the person and acknowledging that he is gone is part of the process of healing.

6. Allow Your Friend to Lead the Conversation or Activity

While it is good to encourage your friend to talk about the death or express her feelings, do not push him if he does not want to. Likewise, while it is good to encourage him to participate in his usual activities, respect his wishes if he does not feel ready. Always meet him at his level of comfort. Do not rush him through the grieving process or expect him to resume normal activities in a short period of time. Grieving takes time and each individual experiences grief differently.

7. Listen

Encourage your friend to talk about the death and express his feelings. Be attentive and accepting of what he has to say. Avoid arguing with him and giving too much advice. It is all right to share some of your own feelings and experiences, but be careful not to spend too much time talking about yourself. Keep your focus on your friend's feelings and experiences.

8. Allow and Acknowledge Expression of Feelings

It is normal for a bereaved person to experience all kinds of feelings. Acknowledge the shock and that your friend is upset, confused and even angry or ashamed. Acknowledging and allowing the expression of anger helps to decrease the intensity of the emotion. Allow your friend to cry and do not limit the crying. It is also normal for a bereaved person to laugh as he recalls happy memories of the deceased or even just to relieve tension. Encourage your friend to express his feelings by writing poems, songs, letters or making a scrapbook.

9. Remove Blame and Guilt

It is normal when a suicide has occurred for survivors to want to find fault or blame someone, be it themselves, someone else or even the deceased. It is human nature to want to find reasons for things we do not understand, but very often there are no simple answers in a suicide. Help your friend to understand that suicide is a very complex matter and there are often multiple stresses in the deceased's life that resulted in the suicide. Avoid making moralistic judgments about the deceased. Blaming another person for the suicide can also be harmful to that person as it may cause unnecessary guilt and self-doubt. Help your friend to understand that regardless of what happened before the suicide or how his relationship with the deceased was before the suicide, he did not cause the suicide and he should not hold himself responsible. The decision to die was made by the deceased and him alone.

10. Reduce Anxiety

When a suicide occurs, teenagers are jolted out of a sense of security and may feel vulnerable. Your friend may worry about the possibility that he too may kill himself or that one of his friends may do so if things get bad enough. Help your friend to see that he is different from the deceased[21] and that he can choose to do things differently. Point out to him that many people have troubles but most people choose other options instead of killing themselves.

11. Engage Your Friend in Activities at his Comfort Level

Some grieving individuals may isolate themselves from others and withdraw from their usual activities. While it is normal for them to do so, it is not helpful when this isolation and withdrawal is prolonged. Prolonged isolation may increase feelings of loneliness, emptiness and alienation, and does not help the person move on with his life. Gently reach out to your friend and encourage him to participate in activities at his comfort level. Offer to attend the wake or funeral of the deceased with him, take him on walks or simply be with him in the comfort of his home, accompanying him on routine activities such as housework, cooking, reading or watching television. If necessary, suggest resources that he could approach for help.

12. Be Alert to Suicidal Thinking and Behaviour

When a suicide occurs, the sense of loss, loneliness, emptiness and other intense emotions that result may lead the ones left behind to think about ending their own lives. Some teenagers who are already wrestling with their own troubles may be influenced into thinking that suicide is also an option for them. Those who are already having thoughts of suicide may be influenced to push ahead with their plans. It is therefore important to be alert to suicidal thinking or behaviour in your friends or peers who have experienced a death by suicide. Pay attention to warning signs and be especially vigilant on anniversary dates such as the deceased's birthday or the date of the suicide. Make it clear to your friend that suicide is never a good solution to problems[21].

13. Offer Resources for Help

If your friend is having difficulties coping with the suicide of someone he knew, do seek help and support from a parent, teacher, school counsellor, pastor or any other adult that you trust. There are also counsellors and therapists who are specially trained to help people cope with the complex feelings and issues that arise from suicide. Your friend can also join a support group where he can meet those who have undergone similar experiences. If your friend finds it difficult to talk to someone face-to-face, there are youth and crisis hotlines that can be a source of support and comfort.

NORMAL GRIEF VERSUS GRIEF COMPLICATIONS

While there is no right or wrong way to grieve, for some people, grieving is prolonged to the point that the person is unable to resume the usual activities of living and carry on with his daily tasks. In such cases, the bereaved is unable to adapt positively to the loss and his ability to go on with life is hindered by his grief. This is unhealthy and he may need professional help.

Certain factors may make the person more vulnerable to problems arising from the grief. These factors include[22, 23]:

- The age of the bereaved. Younger children may be more vulnerable.
- The death of a parent (especially if the death is by suicide).
- A poor relationship between the bereaved and the deceased.
- Sudden and unexpected death.
- The death was the result of terminal illness lasting more than 6 months.
- The death involved disfiguration, mental deterioration or mutilation of the deceased.
- The lack of honest and accurate information given about the death.
- The delay of information about the death for more than one day for a child.
- The loss of a parent and the surviving parent has difficulties coping or mental health problems.
- The gender of the bereaved. Girls or young women are more vulnerable if they have lost someone through childbirth or uterine, ovarian or breast cancer.
- The death causes drastic changes in the economic and social status of the family.
- The bereaved had mental health problems prior to the death.

WHEN DO I NEED ADDITIONAL HELP?

Below are some of the signs that indicate that grieving is not progressing well and that you may need help from a professional trained to deal with such complex issues[2,7]:

- You have thoughts of killing yourself.
- You engage in delinquent behaviour such as truancy or stealing.
- You engage in self-harm behaviour such as the increased use of illicit drugs or alcohol, or engaging in sexual activity with little regard for pregnancy or sexually transmitted diseases.
- You feel out of control and behave aggressively such as fighting with others, destroying things or using abusive language.
- Your schoolwork deteriorates and your grades fall below what you would normally expect.
- You feel a lack of emotion.

- You find yourself expressing emotions that are inappropriate to the situation. For instance, being overly cheerful at the funeral of the deceased.
- You feel restless and find yourself being overly active.
- You find that your personality has changed suddenly such as becoming withdrawn when you used to enjoy socialising with others.
- You withdraw or retreat from social activities.
- You are constantly angry or depressed.
- You are constantly fearful and dependent on others.
- You find it very difficult to be away from people that are important to you.
- You experience physical symptoms such as poor appetite, sleep difficulties, headaches, muscles aches and so on.
- You are not taking good care of yourself.

If you or someone you know exhibits the above signs, do not hesitate to seek help. Talk to an adult or someone you trust about this and ask them to help you or your friend through this difficult period.

HELPLINES AND RESOURCES

Child Guidance Clinic (CGC)

http://www.imh.com.sg/children_guide_clinic.html

The Child Guidance Clinic provides psychological, psychiatric and educational services for children and adolescents up to 19 years of age. Most of the children and adolescents seen by the department do not suffer from mental illness. They have emotional and behavioural problems that require professional help. Children and adolescents can be seen either at the Child Guidance Clinic located at the Health Promotion Board Building or at the Institute of Mental Health. There is also a Child and Adolescent Inpatient Unit at the Institute of Mental Health where children or adolescents who are at high risk for suicide are warded and kept under close supervision around the clock.

Child Guidance Clinic (CGC), Health Promotion Board (HPB)

Second Hospital Avenue, #03-01, Singapore 168937
Enquiries tel. no.: 6389 2200
Operational hours: Mondays to Fridays, 8:00 am to 5:00 pm
Getting there: Bus services 2, 12, 33, 54, 62, 63, 81, 174, 190, 851, 75, 970, 961, 147, 197
Email: hpb@imh.com.sg

Sunrise Wing, Child Guidance Clinic (CGC)
Buangkok Green Medical Park (BGMP)
Block 3, Basement 10, Buangkok View, Singapore 539747
Enquiries tel. no.: 6389 2200
Operational hours: Mondays to Thursdays, 8:00 am to 5:30 pm,
Fridays, 8:00 am to 5:00 pm
Getting there: Bus services 88, 101, 156, 159, 161, 325
Email: imh_appt@imh.com.sg

PSLE Hotline

Helpline: 1800 778 7220
The PSLE Hotline is run by the Student Care Service to meet the needs of students and parents during the weeks before and after the Primary School Leaving Examinations. Primary six students and their parents are encouraged to call the toll-free hotline should they need to talk to a counsellor regarding their anxieties about the examinations.

Tinkle Friend

For children aged 7 to 12
Helpline: 1800 274 4788
www.childrensociety.org.sg
Operational hours: Mondays to Fridays, 9:30 am to 11:30 am, 2:30 pm to 5:00 pm (closed on public holidays)
Tinkle Friends is the Singapore Children's Society toll-free helpline for primary school children. The helpline provides support, advice and information to lonely and distressed children, especially in situations when their parents or main caregivers are unavailable. The Tinkle Friend helpline is manned by trained volunteers.

YouthLine

For youths aged 16 to 20
Helpline: 6336 3434
Operational hours: 9:00 am to 6:00 pm

Samaritans of Singapore

24-hour helpline: 1800 221 4444

http://www.samaritans.org.sg/index1.html

The Samaritans of Singapore aims to prevent suicide by providing emotional support to all persons who are in crisis, thinking of suicide or affected by suicide. It is a non-profit and non-religious organisation which operates on a 24-hour basis.

Family Service Centres

24-hour helpline: 1800 222 0000

http://app.mcys.gov.sg/web/faml_supfaml_familyservicesctr.asp

Family Service Centres are run by voluntary welfare organisations and supported by the Ministry of Community Development, Youth and Sports and the National Council of Social Service. They are located within the community and staffed by professional social workers who are ready to provide a listening ear and helping hand. They have a good network in the community and can help you obtain assistance from other social and community service agencies if necessary. Services are available to anyone, regardless of age, race, language or religion.

Singapore Association for Mental Health

Helpline: 1800 283 7019

http://www.samhealth.org.sg/

Operational hours: Mondays to Fridays, 9:00 am to 6:00 pm

The Singapore Association for Mental Health is a voluntary welfare organisation (non-government and non-profit), which seeks to promote the social and mental well-being of the people of Singapore. It aims to promote mental health, prevent mental illness, improve the care and rehabilitation of persons with mental illness, and to reduce the misconception and social stigma that surround mental illness. It provides face-to-face counselling as well as a toll-free hotline for callers who seek information or help for their concerns.

DepNet
http://www.depnet.com.sg

DepNet is a website that provides advice and information about depression. It also runs an online chat room, forum and diary feature designed to foster communication and interaction among people affected by depression.

Other Websites

http://www.nami.org/helpline/depression-child.html
http://www.aacap.org/publications/factsfam/depressd.htm
http://www.nimh.nih.gov/health/topics/depression/depression-in-children-and-adolescents.shtml

Chapter 1

1. *The Straits Times*, 23 August 2001
2. Lindqvist P, Johansson L, Karlsson U. In the aftermath of teenage suicide: A qualitative study of the psychosocial consequences for the surviving family members. Biomed Central Psychiatry, 8:26. 2008
3. Sveen CA, Walby FA. Suicide survivors' mental health and grief reactions: A systematic review of controlled studies. Suicide and Life Threatening Behaviour, 38(1):13-29. Feb 2008
4. Chia BH. *Too young to die*. Times Editions, 2001
5. Laukkanen E, Honkalampi K, Hintikka J, Hintikka U, Lehtonen J: Suicidal ideation among help-seeking adolescents: association with a negative self-image. Archives of Suicide Research, 9(1):45-55. 2005
6. Ung EK. *Youth suicide and parasuicide in Singapore*. Annals of the Academy of Medicine Singapore, 32(1):12-8. Jan 2003
7. Wong JP, Stewart SM, Ho SY, Rao U, Lam TH. Exposure to suicide and suicidal behaviors among Hong Kong adolescents. Social Science and Medicine, 61(3):591-9. Aug 2005
8. O'Leary CC, Frank DA, Grant-Knight W, Beeghly M, Augustyn M, Rose-Jacobs R, Cabral HJ, Gannon K. Suicidal ideation among urban nine and ten year olds. Journal of Developmental and Behavioural Paediatrics, 27(1):33-9. Feb 2006
9. Liew A, Lim CG, Fung DSS. Suicidal Behaviour in Children and Adolescents–Prevalence and Risk Factors. Submitted manuscript, 2009
10. National Health and Medical Research Council. *Depression in young people: A guide for general practitioners*. Canberra, Australian Government Publishing Service, 1997

Chapter 2

1. Koh JBK, Chang WC, Fung DSS, & Kee CHY. Conceptualization and manifestation of depression in an Asian context: Formal construction and validation of a children's depression scale in Singapore. Culture, Medicine, and Psychiatry, 31: 225-249. 2007
2. Woo BSC, Chang WC, Fung DSS, Koh JBK, Leong JSF, Kee CHY, Seah CKF. Development and validation of a depression scale for Asian adolescents. Journal of Adolescence, 27: 677-689. 2004
3. Woo BSC, Ng TP, Fung DSS, Chan YH, Lee YP, Koh JBK, Cai YM. Emotional

and Behavioural Problems in Singaporean Children Based on Parent, Teacher and Child Reports. Singapore Medical Journal, 48(12):1100–1106. 2007

4. Mahendran R, Yap HL. Clinical practice guidelines for depression. Singapore Medical Journal, 46(11): 610–615. 2005.

5. Chia BH. *Too Young to Die*. Times Editions. 2001.

6. Ghaziuddin N, Kutcher SP, Knapp P, Bernet W, Arnold V, Beitchman J, Benson RS, Bukstein O, Kinlan J, McClellan J, Rue D, Shaw JA, Stock S, Kroeger Ptakowski K; Work Group on Quality Issues; AACAP. Practice parameter for use of electroconvulsive therapy with adolescents. Journal of the American Academy of Child and Adolescent Psychiatry, 43(12):1521–1539. 2004

Chapter 3

1. Luciani JJ: *Self-Coaching: The Powerful Program to Beat Anxiety and Depression*, Wiley. 2nd edition, 2006

2. O'Connor R. *Undoing Depression*. Berkley Trade, 1999

3. Elliott CH, Smith LL, Beck AT. *Anxiety & Depression Workbook For Dummies*. 2005

Chapter 4

1. Tsoi WF, Kua EH. Suicide following parasuicide in Singapore. British Journal of Psychiatry, 151:543-5. Oct 1987

2. Ung EK. Youth suicide and parasuicide in Singapore. Annals of the Academy of Medicine Singapore, 32(1):12-8. Jan 2003

3. Wertheimer A. *A Special Scar: The Experiences of People Bereaved by Suicide*. 2nd edition, Psychology Press, 2001

4. News release: "Suicide huge but preventable public health problem, says WHO", Geneva, 8 September 2004, from World Health Organization website: http://www.who.int/mediacentre/news/releases/2004/pr61/en/

5. Suicide prevention (SUPRE), from World Health Organization website, viewed Oct 2008. http://www.who.int/mental_health/prevention/suicide/suicideprevent/en/index.html

6. Al-Habshi S. Suicide, a preventable public health problem. *Yemen Times*, Issue: (876), Volume 13, From 12 September 2005 to 14 September 2005 http://yementimes.com/article.shtml?i=876&p=health&a=3

7. Nelson ER & Slaikeu KA. Crisis intervention in the schools. In KA Slaikeu (Ed), *Crisis Intervention: A Handbook for Practice and Research*. 2nd edition, 329-347. Boston: Allyn and Bacon, 1990

8. Wass H, Miller MD & Thornton G. Death education and grief/suicide intervention in the public schools. *Death Studies*, 14, 253-268. 1990

9. Shaffer D, Garland AF, Gould M, Fisher P & Trautman P. Preventing teenage suicide: A critical review. *Journal of the American Academy of Child and Adolescent Psychiatry*, 27, 675-687. 1988

10. Hicks BB. *Youth Suicide: A Comprehensive Manual for Prevention and Intervention*. Bloomington, IN: National Educational Service. 1990

11. Kalafat J. *School-Based Youth Suicide Response Programs. Crisis Prevention and Response: A Collection of NASP Resources*. National Association of School Psychologists. 1999

12. Kalafat J & Ryerson DN. The Implementation and Institutionalization of a School-Based Youth Suicide Prevention Program. *The Journal of Primary Prevention*, 19 (3): 157-175. 1999

13. Center for Disease Control. *Youth suicide prevention and resource guide.* Atlanta, GA: Author. 1992

14. Poland S. *Best Practices in Suicide Intervention. Crisis Prevention and Response: A Collection of NASP Resources.* National Association of School Psychologists. 1999

15. Poland S. *Suicide Intervention in the Schools: A Handout for School Personnel. Crisis Prevention and Response: A Collection of NASP Resources.* National Association of School Psychologists. 1999

16. Sowers J. Issues in curriculum and program development. In A McEnvoy (Chair), Suicide Prevention and the Schools. Symposium sponsored by Learning Publications, Orlando, FL. 1987

17. California State Department of Education. *Suicide prevention program for the California public schools.* Sacramento: Author. 1987

18. Preventing suicide: A resource for primary health care workers, World Health Organization, Geneva 2000, WHO/MNH/MBD/00.4, http://www.who.int/mental_health/media/en/62.pdf

19. Weissman MM, Fox K, Klerman GL. Hostility and depression associated with suicide attempts. American journal of psychiatry, 130: 450-455, 1973

20. Erikson EH. *Identity, Youth and Crisis.* New York, Norton, 1994

21. Papenfuss RL et al. Teaching positive self-concepts in the classroom. *Journal of School Health*, 53: 618-620, 1983

22. Malley PB, Kusk F, Bogo RJ. School-based adolescent suicide prevention and intervention programs: a survey. School Counselor, 42: 130-136, 1994

23. Shaffer D, Garland A & Bacon K. Prevention issues in youth suicide (Report prepared for Project Prevention, American Academy of Child and Adolescent Psychiatry). New York: Adolescent Study Unit, College of Physicians and Surgeons of Columbia University. 1987

24. Cliffone J. Suicide prevention: A classroom presentation to adolescents. Social Work, 38, 197-203. 1993

25. Garland AF, Shaffer D & Whittle B. A national survey of school-based adolescent suicide prevention programs. *Journal of the American Academy of Child and Adolescent Psychiatry*, 28, 931-934. 1989

26. Shaffer D, Vieland V, Garland A, Rojas M, Underwood M & Busner C. Adolescent suicide attempters: response to suicide prevention programs. Journal of the American Medical Association, 264, 3151-3155. 1990

27. Centers for Disease Control. *Youth suicide prevention programs: A resource guide.* Atlanta, GA: US Department of Health and Human Services. 1992

28. Garland AF & Zigler E. Adolescent suicide prevention: Current research and social policy implications. *American Psychologist*, 48, 169-182. 1993

29. Brock SE & Sandoval J. S*uicidal Ideation and Behaviours. Crisis Prevention and Response: A Collection of NASP Resources.* National Association of School Psychologists. 1999

30. Smith J. *Coping with Suicide.* New York, Rosen, 1986

31. Hahn WO. *Suicide in Children and Adolescents: Information for Parents. Crisis*

Prevention and Response: A Collection of NASP Resources. National Association of School Psychologists. 1999

32. Barrett T. *Youth in crisis: Seeking solutions to self-destructive behaviour.* Longmont, CO: Sopris West. 1985
33. McBrien J. Are you thinking of killing yourself?: Confronting students' suicidal thoughts. *The School Counselor,* 31 (1), 79-82. 1983
34. Poland. *Suicide Intervention in the Schools.* New York: Guilford. 1989
35. Davis JM & Sandoval J. *Suicidal Youth: School-Based Intervention and Prevention.* San Francisco: Jossey-Bass. 1991
36. Mauk GW & Sharpnack JD. *Grief. Crisis Prevention and Response: A Collection of NASP Resources.* National Association of School Psychologists. 1999
37. Kneisel D & Richards G. Crisis intervention after the suicide of a teacher. *Professional Psychology: Research and Practice,* 19(2), 165-169. 1988
38. Lamb F & Dunne-Maxim K. Postvention in the schools: Policy and process. In E Dunne, J McIntosh & K Dunne-Maxim (Eds), Suicide and its Aftermath, 245-263. New York: Norton. 1987
39. Leenaars A & Wenckstern S. *Suicide prevention in schools.* New York: Hemisphere. 1991
40. Lamartine C. Suicide prevention in educational settings. In After a Suicide Death (pamphlet). Dayton, OH: Suicide Prevention Centre. 1985
41. Thompson R. Suicide and sudden loss: Crisis management in the schools. Highlights: An ERIC/CAPS digest, 1. 1990
42. Ruof SR & Harris JM. Suicide contagion: Guilt and modeling. Communique, 16(7), 8. 1988
43. Davidson LE. Suicide cluster and youth. In CR Pfeffer (Ed), Suicide Among Youth: Perspectives on Risk and Prevention (pp. 83-99) Washington DC: American Psychiatric Press. 1989
44. Berman AL & Jobes DA. *Adolescent suicide: Assessment and intervention.* Washington DC: American Psychological Association. 1991
45. Wenckstern S & Leenaars AA. Trauma and suicide in our schools. *Death Studies,* 17, 151-171. 1993
46. Brock SE, Sandoval J & Lewis S. *Preparing for crises in the schools: A manual for building school crisis response teams.* Brandon, VT: Clinical Psychology Publishing, 1996
47. Sandoval, J, & Brock, SE. The school psychologist's role in suicide prevention. School Psychology Quarterly, 11, 169-185. 1996

Chapter 5

1. Garland AF & Zigler E. Adolescent suicide prevention: Current research and social policy implications. American Psychologist, 48, 169-182. 1993
2. Brent DA, Baugher M, Bridge J, Chen T, Chiapptta L. Age- and sex-related risk factors for adolescent suicide. Journal of the American Academy of Child and Adolescent Psychiatry 38:1497-1505. 1999
3. Ung EK. Youth suicide and parasuicide in Singapore. Annals of the Academy of Medicine Singapore, 32, 12-18. 2003
4. American Psychiatric Association. *Diagnostic and statistical manual of mental disorders.* Fourth edition. Washington, DC:Author. 1994

5. Brock SE & Sandoval J. Suicidal Ideation and Behaviours. *Crisis Prevention and Response: A Collection of NASP Resources.* National Association of School Psychologists. 1999

6. Ramsay RF, Tanney BL, Tierney RJ & Lang WA. *The California Helper's Handbook for suicide intervention.* Sacramento, CA: State Department of Mental Health. Primary Consultants, 1990

7. Hahn WO. *Suicide in Children and Adolescents: Information for Parents. Crisis Prevention and Response: A Collection of NASP Resources.* National Association of School Psychologists. 1999

8. Preventing suicide: A resource for primary health care workers, World Health Organization, Geneva 2000, WHO/MNH/MBD/00.4, http://www.who.int/mental_health/media/en/62.pdf

9. Maine Teen Suicide Prevention: I'm worried about myself, Maine Youth Suicide Prevention Program, Dept of Health and Human Services, State of Maine, 2006, http://maine.gov/suicide/youth/myself/index.htm

10. Maine Teen Suicide Prevention: I'm worried about a friend, Maine Youth Suicide Prevention Program, Dept of Health and Human Services, State of Maine, 2006, http://maine.gov/suicide/youth/friend/index.htm

11. Moscicki EK (1995). Epidemiology of suicidal behaviour. Suicide and Life-Threatening Behaviour, 25, 22-35

Chapter 6

1. *The Straits Times*, 6 October 2008

2. Mauk GW & Sharpnack JD. Grief. Crisis Prevention and Response: A Collection of NASP Resources. National Association of School Psychologists. 1999

3. For Parents: Common Youth Reactions to Suicide, Maine Youth Suicide Prevention Program, Dept of Health and Human Services, State of Maine, 2006, http://maine.gov/suicide/parents/common.htm

4. Wertheimer A. A Special Scar: The Experiences of People Bereaved by Suicide. Second edition, Psychology Press. 2001

5. For Parents: Am I Normal?, Maine Youth Suicide Prevention Program, Dept of Health and Human Services, State of Maine, 2006 http://maine.gov/suicide/parents/normal.htm

6. List of guidelines for health emergency: Posttraumatic stress disorder (PTSD), World Health Organization (WHO), last update 9 Oct 2006, http://www.searo.who.int/en/Section1257/Section2263/Section2310/Section2320_12480.htm

7. Beckman R. *Children who Grieve: A Manual for Conducting Support Groups.* Holmes Beach, FL: Learning Publications. 1990

8. Sims D. A model for grief intervention and death education in the public schools. In JD Morgan (Ed), Young People and Death, 185-190. Philadelphia: the Charles press. 1991

9. Rando TA. What is grief? In TA Rando (Ed), Grieving: How to Go On Living When Someone You Love Dies, 18-23. Lexington MA: Lexington Books. 1988

10. Saunders JM. A process of bereavement resolution: Uncoupled identity. Western Journal of Nursing Research, 3, 319-322. 1981

11. Fox SS. Good grief: Preventive interventions for children and adolescents. In SC Klagsbrun, GW Kliman, EJ Clark, AH Kutscher, R DeBellis & CA Lambert (Eds), Preventive Psychiatry: Early Intervention and Situations Crisis Management, 83-93. Philadelphia: The Charles Press. 1989

12. Doka KJ. Disenfranchised grief. In KJ Doka (Ed), Disenfranchised Grief: Recognizing Hidden Sorrow, 3-11. Lexington MA: DC Health. 1989

13. Mauk GW & Weber C. Peer survivors of adolescent suicide: Perspectives on grieving and postvention. Journal of Adolescent Research, 6, 113-131. 1991

14. Osterweis M, Solomon F & Green M (Eds). *Bereavement: Reactions, Consequences and Care.* Washington DC: National Academy Press. 1984

15. Everstine DS & Everstine L. *The Trauma Response: Treatment for Emotional Injury.* New York: WW Norton. 1993

16. O'Carroll P. Suicide prevention: clusters and contagion. In AL Berman (Ed), Suicide Prevention: Case Consultations, 25-55. New York: Springer. 1990

17. For Youth: When a friend dies by suicide, Maine Youth Suicide Prevention Program, Dept of Health and Human Services, State of Maine, 2006, http://maine.gov/suicide/youth/friend/dies.htm

18. For Parents: After a youth suicide, Maine Youth Suicide Prevention Program, Dept of Health and Human Services, State of Maine, 2006, http://maine.gov/suicide/parents/after.htm

19. Nock, MK, About Teen Suicide, KidsHealth, Nemours Foundation, Reviewed June 2008, http://kidshealth.org/parent/emotions/behavior/suicide.html

20. For Parents: How to support grieving youth, Maine Youth Suicide Prevention Program, Dept of Health and Human Services, State of Maine, 2006, http://maine.gov/suicide/parents/support.htm

21. Ruof SR & Harris JM. Suicide contagion: Guilt and modeling. Communique, 16(7), 8. 1988

22. Osterweis M & Townsend J. *Helping Bereaved Children: A Booklet for School Personnel.* Rockville, MD: US Department of Health and Human Services, National Institute of Mental Health. 1988

23. Kliman G. *Psychological Emergencies of Childhood.* New York: Grune and Stratton. 1968

DR DANIEL FUNG is Chief of the Department of Child and Adolescent Psychiatry at the Institute of Mental Health where he is also the Director of Clinical Quality. He is an Adjunct Associate Professor with the Duke-NUS Graduate Medical School and the Division of Psychology, School of Humanities and Social Sciences at Nanyang Technological University.

Dr Fung received several awards including the PS 21 Star Service Award in 2009, National Council of Social Services long service award in 2008 and the Singapore Children's Society Silver Service Award in 2007. In 2000, Dr Fung was awarded the Ministry of Health's Health Manpower Development Plan Fellowship at the Hospital for Sick Children, Toronto and he completed a Clinical Research Fellowship the same year.

He is vice-chairman of the Clinical Research Committee in IMH and is a principal investigator and co-investigator for various studies on clinical interventions for behaviour and anxiety disorders.

Dr Fung has authored and co-authored numerous publications ranging from academic works to stories about his life, work and medicine in general. Among the books he has written is one entitled *Help Your Child to Cope: Understanding Childhood Stress*. He also wrote a textbook on childhood and adolescent psychiatry for trainee doctors.

A dedicated doctor with a soft spot for children, Dr Fung is married to Joyce and has five wonderful children, Grace, Joelle, Deborah, Louisa May and Peter Joseph.

CAROLYN KEE is a Senior Psychologist with the Department of Child and Adolescent Psychiatry at the Institute of Mental Health. She has a Masters in Child and Adolescent Mental Health from the Institute of Psychiatry, London, and a post-graduate diploma in Satir Brief Systemic Therapy.

Ms Kee has participated in various research projects and contributed articles to scientific journals and magazines as well as chapters to books on mental health issues. She has also authored and co-authored storybooks for parents and children. As a psychologist, she has worked with parents and children, and is humbled and inspired by the stories of those who struggle daily to overcome their problems and difficulties. She has two lovely daughters of her own and is grateful to experience fully the anxieties, challenges, joys and rewards of parenthood.

DR REBECCA P ANG is currently an Associate Professor at Division of Psychology, School of Humanities and Social Sciences, Nanyang Technological University. She obtained her PhD in school psychology (specialising in clinical child psychology) from Texas A&M University. Her research and professional interests include developmental child psychopathology and interventions for children and adolescents at-risk for behavioural and emotional disorders.

Dr Ang received the School Psychology Review Outstanding Article of the Year Award in 2002 from the National Association of School Psychologists, USA. This award was given in recognition of outstanding research advancing the field of school psychology. In 2004, she received the Japanese Chamber of Commerce and Industry (JCCI) Singapore Foundation Education Award in recognition of work in psychology, and for advancing the education of at-risk children and youth in Singapore. In addition to her research, she is active in public and social service in Singapore, having been invited to sit on various government and non-government advisory committees where she contributes towards shaping policies in the areas of education, counseling and mental health.